MW01169432

Diary of an Enderman Ninja

An Unofficial Minecraft Series

Books 1-3
FULL ELIAS TRILOGY

Diary of an Enderman Ninja – Book 1
Diary of an Enderman Ninja – Book 2
Diary of an Enderman Ninja – Book 3
Skeleton Steve

www.SkeletonSteve.com

Copyright

"Diary of an Enderman Ninja Trilogy"

"Diary of an Enderman Ninja – Book 1"

"Diary of an Enderman Ninja – Book 2"

"Diary of an Enderman Ninja – Book 3"

Copyright © 2017, Lightbringer Media LLC, All Rights Reserved

www.SkeletonSteve.com

Disclaimer: This unofficial novel is an original work of fan fiction; it is not an official Minecraft book. It is not endorsed, authorized, sanctioned, approved, licensed, sponsored, or supported by Mojang AB, Microsoft Corp. or any other entity owning or controlling rights to the Minecraft name, trademarks, or copyrights.

Minecraft®/ TM & © 2009-2017 Mojang / Notch / Microsoft

All names, places, characters, and all other aspects of the game mentioned from here on are trademarks or company names mentioned in this book are the property of their respective owners and are only mentioned for identification purposes.

EBooks are not transferable. No part of this book may be used or reproduced in any manner without written permission, except in the case of brief quotations embodied in critical articles and reviews. The unauthorized reproduction or distribution of this copyrighted work is illegal. No part of this book may be scanned, uploaded, or distributed via the Internet or any other means, electronic or print, without the publisher's permission.

Published in the United States of America by Lightbringer Media LLC, 2017

To join Skeleton Steve's free mailing list, for updates about new Minecraft Fanfiction titles:

www.SkeletonSteve.com

Table of Contents

Contents

Book Introduction by Skeleton Steve

Love MINECRAFT? **Over 63,000 words of kid-friendly fun!**

This high-quality fan fiction fantasy diary book is for kids, teens, and nerdy grown-ups who love to read epic stories about their favorite game!

Thank you to <u>all</u> of you who are buying and reading my books and helping me grow as a writer. I put many hours into writing and preparing this for you. I *love* Minecraft, and writing about it is almost as much fun as playing it. It's because of *you*, reader, that I'm able to keep writing these books for you and others to enjoy.

This book is dedicated to *you*. Enjoy!!

After you read this book, please take a minute to leave a simple review. I really appreciate the feedback from my readers, and love to read your reactions to my stories, good or bad. If you ever want to see your name/handle featured in one of my stories, leave a review and *tell me about it* in there! And if you ever want to ask me any questions, or tell me your idea for a cool Minecraft story, you can email me at steve@skeletonsteve.com.

Are you on my **Amazing Reader List**? Find out at the end of the book!

September the 21st, 2016

For those of you who love Elias the Enderman Ninja and like a good deal, enjoy this Box Set! If you'd like to see me continue the adventures of Elias, LuckyMist, Xenocide99, and WolfBroJake, please let me know in the comments!

- Skeleton Steve

P.S. - Have you joined the Skeleton Steve Club and my Mailing List?? *Check online to learn how!*

You found one of my diaries!!

This is a BUNDLE OF STORIES of one of my friends, Cth'ka the creeper—a *true hero* of Diamodia. You are holding the first *box set* collection of diary entries from his journey of becoming a great king of *creeperkind!*

Be warned—this is an *epic book!* You're going to *care* about these characters. You'll be scared for them, feel good for them, and feel bad for them! It's my hope that you'll be *sucked up* into the story, and the adventure and danger will be so intense, you'll forget we started this journey with a *video game!*

So with that, dear reader, I present to you the tale of **Elias the Enderman Ninja**, the **Box Set**...

Attention New Readers!!

Go to **SkeletonSteve.com** to get

THESE FOUR FREE GIFTS!

**Three <u>Unique</u> Books about my own
Personal Tips and Tricks in Minecraft
AND One of my Diary _Fiction_ Books!**

Box Set Book 1:
Diary of an Enderman Ninja

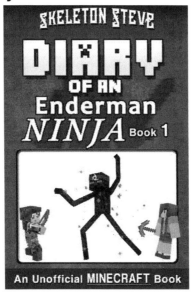

Elias was a young Enderman. And he was a NINJA.

As an initiate of the Order of the Warping Fist, Elias is sent on a mission by his master to investigate the deaths of several Endermen at Nexus 426. Elias is excited to prove himself as a novice martial artist, but is a little nervous--he still hasn't figured out how to dodge arrows!

And now, when the young Enderman ninja discovers that the source of the problem is a trio of tough, experienced Minecraftian players, will he be in over his head? And what's this talk about a 'Skeleton King' and an army of undead?

Day 1 - Overworld

When I teleported to the Overworld, I never thought that I would be starting a *diary*.

It is always interesting, the adventures that life puts in my path. So here I am, an Enderman, sitting on a rock and penning words into this empty book I found in a chest.

The day is clear today. Warm. Very pleasant.

It feels strange, trying to think of things to say with my fingers instead of with my mind, to use this archaic quill and ink to put words on paper.

The grass, and the leaves in the trees, are swaying and whispering in the wind, as I scratch these words onto paper in this leather-bound book resting on my lap.

Such is the way.

I am reminded frequently by the flow of the world around me to ignore my expectations, because once I expect something to go *one* way,

7

the universe opens like a flower and teases me into another direction.

But I am ninja, so I flow like water.

Or, at least, I *try* to.

So I embrace this journal. This diary.

I will write of my adventures on my *Seed Stride*, and it will become part of my way. A painting of this path on my journey of life.

My name is Elias, and I am Ender.

I am also an initiate in the Order of the Warping Fist—a unique group of Endermen *ninja*. By now, I would have normally been granted the title of 'lower ninja', but the end of my initiate training was interrupted by the Seed Stride.

It occurs to me that writing this diary gives life to my story, and my story may travel on away from me once it has life. One day, my story and I may go separate ways—my body and my words separate, but together.

So I must explain.

The 'Seed Stride' is a rite of passage for young Endermen. Just before we reach adulthood and become full members of the Ender race, we are compelled to go on a Seed Stride. This is the first of many Seed Strides I will take over the course of my life, to help contribute to the well-being and expansion of my people.

We Ender, as a race, rely on the Pearls, our *Chi*, to produce more Ender, and to attune ourselves to the rhythm of the universe. Our Chi is also the source of our power to teleport, to warp between worlds, and also enhances our ability to communicate by the voice of the mind.

Such things we Ender take for granted. But it is possible that *you*, whoever picks up this book, as my story decides to *travel* later, may not understand the simple concepts that I've known since my birth.

So, now that you understand, *know* that my first Seed Stride was the reason my initiate ninja training was interrupted before completion.

Mature Endermen all understand, either through training or experience, how to dodge arrows and other missile weapons through the awareness they achieve by being in tune with their *Chi* and the world around them.

I'm still working on it.

When it was time to begin my Seed Stride, I was a little concerned that I hadn't yet mastered the Chi dodge, but as a ninja, I am comfortable enough in my combat ability to make up for my lack of skill in Chi.

Once my Seed Stride is complete, I will return to my master to complete my training. Then, I will increase in rank to lower ninja and start participating in real missions.

I understand that I am supposed to control my emotions. But the idea of finally being a real ninja and going on missions for the Order excites me! I'm sure that such excitement clouds my mind with impatience...

But I've got that impatience under control—really, I do!

So, I mentioned that the Ender people rely on the pearls. The pearls are the source of our enhanced power; the technology of our race.

I received my Ender pearl when I was very small. After going through the trials like all Ender younglings, I was chosen for the order. Some Endermen are more naturally in tune with their Chi than others. My connection and potential showed that I would be one of the few chosen to protect and further the race.

And now, I was almost fully-grown.

Though I recognize the value of humility, I was confident in my strengths.

I'm strong. And fast. And my martial arts skill is among the highest in my class.

I was sure that my connection with my Chi would catch up.

But I was out of time.

The time of my Seed Stride had come, so my training was paused, and now I am sitting on a rock in the sun, being one with the wind and the grass, and writing in this book...

Earlier today, I found a jungle.

The tall, green trees and lush ground was a most interesting biome! There were pools of water here and there, and I realized that a place so green had to experience frequent rain.

Warping through the environment, searching for pearl seeds in the dirt under thick vegetation, I knew that I needed to stay sharp—I wouldn't want to get caught in the rain!

But it didn't rain.

And I found *four* pearl seeds in dirt blocks during the time I traveled and warped through the interesting and lush environment. Trying to sense the Ender energy within, I picked up and discarded block after block of dirt until I could feel the pull of the Chi inside.

Whenever I found a dirt block containing a pearl seed, I opened my dimensional pocket, and stored the block with the other seed blocks for my return home.

The dirt blocks I collected would stay inside the dimensional pocket until I returned to the End at the completion of my Seed Stride.

There was no requirement or limit on the amount of blocks an Enderman was expected to collect on a Seed Stride. Finding the pearl seeds for our people was something engrained in us from an early age—something we were expected to do as a service to our race.

I figured that I would know when I had collected enough seeds. My heart was open, and I would listen to my instinct. Once I finished this Seed Stride, and was satisfied with my service to the Ender people, I would return to the End to plant my seeds and continue my ninja training.

Some Endermen collected more seeds than others. And some dedicated their *entire lives* to the Seed Stride, walking the Overworld forever in search of the dirt blocks that held the promise of a growing pearl.

I would work hard, and collect many seeds. My life as a member of the Order was sworn to a duty to the people, after all. But my real goals lay in the path to becoming a better ninja.

I loved being a ninja. And once I rose to the rank of a lower ninja, I would at least have the respect of my peers.

Yes, maybe I suffered from a *little* bit of pride. I was aware.

But I knew what I wanted.

I wanted to be the best.

The strongest and fastest ninja. I wanted to be a shadow. In time, I hoped that I could even become a master, and be able to channel my Chi into fireballs, and do all of the other cool ninja stuff that Master Ee-Char could do.

So far, I had twenty-seven seeds. Pausing to peer into my dimensional pocket, I counted them again. Twenty-seven blocks of dirt, all holding the promise of growing an Ender pearl to be joined with twenty-seven Ender younglings in the future. Perhaps one of them would also become a ninja, like me.

When I was in the jungle, earlier today, I found an old structure. Old for *Minecraftians*, I guess.

The small building was made of chiseled stone blocks, now overrun with vines and green moss.

As I explored the inside of the old Minecraftian structure, I noted that it was some sort of *temple*. My ninja awareness easily detected a couple of rotting, crude traps, and I avoided the trip lines and pressure plates without effort.

Inside a wooden chest, among a bunch of Minecraftian junk and zombie meat, I found *this book*.

Out of curiosity, I experimented with the levers by the stairs, until I revealed a hidden room with another wooden chest. Just more junk. Pieces of metal and bones.

Those Minecraftians and their junk...

At least, I *figured* it was Minecraftian junk. I had never personally *met* one of the creatures before. From what I'd heard in my training and

15

tales from other Endermen, the Minecraftians were small and weak, but were intelligent, and were able to transform the Overworld into tools, armor, and other technology that made them stronger.

The older Endermen told me stories about the famous *Steve*, as well as other Minecraftians that came and went frequently on the Overworld. We even saw a Minecraftian or two appear every once and a while on the dragon's island, stuck on our world because of dabbling with portal technology they didn't understand. I've never seen them myself, but I've heard about the incidents from Endermen who were there at the time.

Usually, the visiting Minecraftians had it out for the dragon.

It never lasted long.

Apparently, they were usually surprised when they appeared on the obsidian receiver, and realized that there was no way to get home! I've heard that when they inevitably decide to attack the dragon, the great, ancient beast just *plucks them up* and throws them out into the void.

Well, now I had a piece of their junk. This book was constructed from leather and paper, which was likely constructed from something else. This ink was created by Minecraftians as well—all components derived from plants, animals, and minerals of the Overworld, to be sure.

What a beautiful day!

This Overworld is very bright during the day—uncomfortably so. But it's very peaceful and loely.

I think I'll meditate for a while and write more tomorrow...

Day 2 - Overworld

After meditating, filling my Chi, and exploring the Overworld during the night, I decided to stay out in the open again during the next day.

I ran into another couple of Endermen during the night, a time when exploring is a lot easier on our eyes. But now, during the day, now that the sunlight is flooding the world around me, I'm all alone again.

During my training, I was never told to only go out at night, but it seems to be an unspoken rule of my people on the Seed Stride here. And I can understand why. The sun was so bright and hot on my eyes! But I didn't care. Let the others go into hiding or warp back to the End during the day. I had *seeds* to collect and an infinite world to explore!

Today, I observed the animals and the Overworld's native mobs.

There were several different kinds of beasts that I found, as I teleported from valley to valley,

19

hillside to hillside, as the sky lightened with the rising sun. White, clucking birds, fluffy sheep, spotted cows, pink pigs. I was able to understand them by using my Chi to perceive their thoughts, but their language was very basic and they mostly communicated with each other through grunts and noises.

"*What is your name?*" I asked a particular chicken with my *mind voice*.

"*I am a chicken,*" it thought back. "Bawk!" it said aloud.

"*What is your purpose?*"

"*I am eating.*"

The bird scratched at the ground with its goofy yellow feet, pulling plant seeds out of the tall grass.

As the morning went on, I noticed that some of the larger, more complicated creatures, the *mobs*, as I was taught they were called, *burst* into flames as the sun settled higher into the sky! Skeletons and zombies raced around, frantic and on fire, until they burned up and left behind nothing but piles of ash, bones, and charred meat.

What an interesting world.

As I teleported into the shadows of a tall, dark forest, I found a lone zombie hiding from the sun under a pine tree. He held a metal shovel in his hand—a Minecraftian tool.

"*Excuse me,*" I said into his mind.

"Who...? Who's there?" the zombie asked in a dull, slow voice. The creature looked around with black eyes.

I stepped out from the shadows to where it couldn't help but notice me. It's not like I was *trying* to hide before—I don't know how it didn't see me.

The zombie's face stretched in surprise. "Oh!" it cried. "You surprised me! So sneaky!" It settled down, paused, and stood vacant for a moment before speaking again. "What you want?"

"*I was wondering ... why does the sun sets zombies on fire?*" I said into its mind.

The zombie was shocked. "The sun sets zombies on *fire?!*" It was suddenly very aware of the sunlight just outside of the shadow of the tree, and the poor undead creature clutched at the pine's trunk to keep away from the light.

"*Elias,*" I suddenly heard in my mind. The voice of another Enderman. "*Behind you.*"

Turning, I saw, across a sunny valley, was an area of deep shadow under a cliff—probably a cave. Another Enderman stood inside. From here, I could see his eyes glowing purple in the dark, and I could barely make out the white symbol of the *Order of the Warping Fist* on his black headband.

Another ninja.

I left the zombie, teleporting across the valley to stand before the other Enderman.

"*What is it, sir?*" I asked. It was Erion, a lower ninja from the rank just above me. He had finished his initial training, and would now be expected to perform minor missions while still taking training from his master. His headband was black instead of blue (like mine), but still bore the white symbol of a novice.

Soon I would have a black headband like his.

"Elias, you have been summoned by Master Ee'char. He has ordered that you return to the Temple immediately."

"But ... my Seed Stride...?"

"Master Ee'char is aware that you are on Seed Stride. He has sent me to find you and ask you to return to him, still." Erion broke eye contact for a moment, and glared around at the sunny valley. *"What are you doing exploring during the day?"*

"Thank you, Erion. I'll return directly," I said into his mind.

The other Enderman ninja nodded, then disappeared with a *zip* and a brief shower of tiny, purple motes of light.

I turned, and noticed that the zombie I was talking to was gone. In front of the tree, outside of the shadow and in the sunlight, was a pile of charred meat … and a shovel.

Huh.

What a strange world.

Teleporting around on a single world was easy. It was a lot like making a long jump—didn't require much energy, much of my *Chi*. I could overdo it, of course. If I warped around too much in too short a period of time, I would … get tired, in a way. If my energy became too low, I would have to wait, or meditate for a while, until I had enough Chi to teleport again.

While exploring during my Seed Stride, the more I practiced harnessing my Chi for warping, the more I could do it without resting. I suppose there would come a time when teleporting on one world like I did here—hill to hill, place to place— would become as easy as blinking my eyes. In time.

But not yet. I still had to try. Still had to focus. And I could still get tired.

Teleporting was easier today than it was yesterday, though. With practice, I'd be able to

24

warp more without resting and recharging my Chi—I was sure of it!

Jumping to another world was a different matter, however.

Going back and forth between the Overworld and the End was difficult, and required me to focus and have very strong *Chi*. The act needed *all* of my energy. And I'd probably need to recharge quite a bit before I could do it again.

So I sat on the cool stone in the shadow of the cave mouth, my legs crossed, my hands open and resting on my knees, receptive to the Overworld's Ender energy.

I meditated for a while, and let my thoughts dissipate. Focused only on my breathing, I willed my body to be a *receiver* for the energy of the world—the combined energy of all of the pearl seeds hidden in the blocks around me … the energy of the world's core. It all funneled into me, moving up my arms, my legs, spiraling to my center … to my *Chi*.

My Ender pearl was warm inside of me.

And I warped home.

Day 2 – The End

Appearing in the End was an immediate relief to my eyes. The world was dark and pleasant. All was quiet except for the faint flapping of the dragon's wings, its occasional grumbles, and the subtle *zip* sounds of the Ender people warping around.

I appeared on the dragon's island, just like most of us did. It was the easiest place for me to focus on in my mind.

The silence of the void outside of the island was like a heavy embrace.

Endermen bustled around, chatting with each other with their *mind voices*, moving their dirt blocks around, planting seeds.

Focusing next on the Temple of the Order of the Warping Fist, far across the void from the dragon island, I teleported to the outer ring.

Zip.

Appearing just outside the temple, I looked around, shocked at how different the Overworld was from my home. The End was comfortable and consistent. The same meteor-like stone made all of the islands and outliers, and the chorus fruit grew tall and still. There was no wind here. Not really. Not like on the Overworld. Over the last few days, I had grown accustomed to the trees, grass, and the whole world *moving* around me all of the time.

The End was so simple compared to the variety and chaos of the Overworld. Comforting, yes. But the adventure and unknown aspect I'd been seeing in the Overworld was … growing on me.

Outside the temple, I saw another ninja sitting on the bridge, meditating. His eyes were closed, and he kept them closed as I approached. As the Enderman sat, straight and in perfect meditation posture, serene and still, I saw that he was wounded. Several gashes striped his body and left arm. He was clearly trying to channel his *Chi* to heal himself as quickly as possible.

On his forehead was the black headband and red symbol of a middle ninja. A grown adult, fully trained, responsible, and going on normal missions.

"Be well, brother," he said into my head as I drew near.

"What happened to you, sir?" I asked.

"One cannot defeat every opponent," he responded. *"This battle was to be a lesson for me instead of a victory, it seems..."*

"What weapon did that to you?"

"Not the weapon, initiate," he responded. *"The weapon is just a tool. It was a pair of Minecraftians that outmaneuvered me on Overworld. Their tools were diamond swords."*

"You teleported back here to heal?" I asked.

"Yes," the ninja responded. *"The simple Chi of the End makes it easier to focus and attain wholeness."*

I contemplated that for a moment. *"Be well,"* I said. *"Get better."*

The middle ninja nodded, his eyes still closed, and I proceeded across the purpur bridge into the Temple. The Shulker guards pried their shells open for a moment to regard me with beady little eyes, then closed again with a *chunk*.

After teleporting up the main tower, I arrived at the primary dojo, and scanned the crowd of younglings for my master. Two other masters were present and teaching the Ender young. Small Ender bodies struggled and clashed together, and I heard the frequent *zip, zip, zip* of them teleporting around. One of the masters looked up at me from across the big, open room.

"*Initiate Elias,*" he said in my mind, his mind voice as clear as a bell. "*Your master is on the roof.*"

I nodded, and teleported to the base of the stairs. After a brisk walk up the skinny staircase, I emerged under the open void of the End and spotted my master across the huge, flat, purple roof.

Master Ee'char was an old Enderman. Not weakened by age at all, he stood tall and regal on the exposed roof, the highest point of the Order

Temple. The *vast* purple and speckled void swam across the sky above us, reminding me of how small even the Order of the Warping Fist was in the immensity of *the End*. My master turned to me, and I saw his green eyes glow across the dim space.

There were very few Endermen that still had the green eyes from back when our race was young. Other masters, and the elders of the normal Ender population, showed green eyes here and there, but my race's eyes have been *purple* ever since even before the discovery of the *outer rim* and the construction of our great *End Cities*.

"Initiate Elias," my master said in my mind. He turned, and I saw that he held a flower pot from the Overworld in his hand. A tall, red flower grew out of its soil. The red petals were shockingly bright compared to the low light and muted colors of *the End*.

Other flower pots full of Overworld flowers sat on the roof floor behind him, organized in a line. He must have been tending to them when I arrived.

"*Yes, Master?*" I responded, and approached on foot.

"*How goes your Seed Stride?*" Master Ee'char asked, his green eyes focused on the flower. He cleaned dirt and dust from the plant with his nimble black fingers.

"*Going well, master,*" I said. "*I have acquired twenty-seven seeds, and I expect to acquire many more. Why have you summoned me away from the Stride?*"

My master looked up at me, as if shocked by my directness. Or maybe he was faking—I could never read him fully. He slowly turned his attention back to the red flower.

"*What do you see, Elias?*"

"*A red flower from the Overworld,*" I said.

"*And what can you learn from this flower?*"

I thought for a moment about what he might be getting at before responding. "*The flower is strong and is surviving on our world?*"

Master smiled, and turned.

32

"*That is a valid observation,*" he said. "*You may also note its beauty and its symbol of hope, as it struggles in its young life to rise up out of the dirt and muck. This particular plant can only produce flowers if it has enough dirt to push roots through. There is more to this flower than strength and beauty, and you are to contemplate this while you are on your mission...*"

"*What mission?*" I asked. "*Back to my Seed Stride?*"

"*No, young initiate.*" Master Ee'char placed the flower pot gently back onto the purpur roof, then turned to face me, his hands calmly drawn together. "*I am sending you on a mission to investigate an incident developing near Nexus 426.*"

The *Nexus* he was referring to was one of the common areas that we Enderman use to teleport down to the Overworld. When warping to one of the other worlds, we could choose to either appear in a random location, or to focus on a particular location according to memory and experience, *or* to use a common *Nexus* that the Ender race catalogued over time.

Nexus 426 would be one of my peoples' many common warping destinations.

Personally, I'd never been there before...

"*But Master,*" I said, "*What about my Seed Stride?*"

"*Consider this a small diversion, young one,*" he responded. "*Your Seed Stride will still be there for you. The seeds will still be present and waiting for you—even around Nexus 426.*" My master sighed in my mind, then looked out into the void. "*In the last several days, many non-Order Endermen have been killed near that Nexus point. You are to travel there and investigate. And if you can identify the cause of the Ender deaths, you are to neutralize it...*"

A real mission? To assassinate an assassin? But I wasn't even *lower ninja* yet!

"*Respectfully, my master,*" I said, "*why have I been chosen for this? I haven't even finished my initiate training...?*"

Master Ee'char turned back to me, considered my expression, then smiled, bent, and picked a red flower from the flower pots at his feet. He extended the flower to me, and I took it.

"Young initiate, return to the dragon island and plant the seeds you already have. Then teleport to Nexus 426."

I bowed.

"Thank you, master."

The ancient Enderman smiled and turned away, back to his flowers. I departed on foot until I was on the stairs, then placed the red flower into my dimensional pocket and teleported away.

Back on the dragon island, I found a ragged edge of the landmass that was being expanded.

Yes, I thought. *This would do*.

Reaching into my dimensional pocket, I removed my seed blocks, and began adding them to the island, one by one. The dirt blocks bound to the endstone easily, and my meager twenty-seven blocks became a new piece of the island. In time, these seed blocks would transform into endstone, and the dragon's energy would start growing the pearls inside of them.

After spending a moment looking over my handiwork with satisfaction, I warped over to the Gateway, focused on Nexus 426, then teleported back to Overworld.

Day 3 – Overworld

The Overworld was bright.

Focusing on Nexus 426 warped me right into the middle of a desert biome, and it was the middle of the day when I arrived. After the pleasant, dim light of the End, my eyes were assaulted by the glare of the desert sun.

After getting my bearings and looking around, I skipped across the desert with short teleports until I reached the edge of a forest, and found relief just inside the shadowy tree line.

The world was quiet around me. All I could hear was the sound of the wind, and many small, tan rabbits hopping around in the sand outside of the trees.

I had to remind myself that a killer of Endermen was lurking around here somewhere...

Sticking to the shadows, I began warping around the edges of the desert, staying in the trees where I could. Around the large desert was a forest on one side, a grassland on the other. Between the two bordering biomes was a tall mountain made almost entirely of stone. The grasslands extended away from the desert as a far as I could see, transitioning into short hills and plateaus full of animals.

Within the trees, I didn't see many mobs that I could talk to. It was likely that whatever skeletons and zombies were here had already burned up by now, if they didn't find shelter first. Warping around looking for intelligent life, I eventually found a single creeper casually making its way through the woods. Its pale, green body blended in with the grass, and it moved almost as quietly as a ninja.

Almost, I thought. I could still hear its footsteps.

I appeared before the green mob, and it stopped, face pulled into a frown.

"Greetings, creeper," I said into its mind. *"I need a word."*

The creeper craned its neck to look up at me.

"Yesss?" it asked in a raspy, hissing voice. "What isss it, Ender?"

"I am investigating the deaths of my people in this area. Do you know anything about it? Anything odd going on around here?"

"Sss …" it said, thinking to itself. I could read in its body language that it was not happy about being interrupted on its walk, but it seemed to be *afraid* of being difficult with me. "I know little about thisss area. I'm jussst passsing through…"

"You haven't heard anything about your own kind being killed here? Or other mobs?"

"No, Ender. But there isss a mountain to the sssouth! Likely you can find othersss that live here in the cavesss…"

It was referring to the mountain I saw on the edge of the desert between the forest and the grasslands. Yes, a mountain like that was probably *full* of caves and passages! That would be where most of the undead go to hide from the sun during the day.

"Thank you, creeper."

The creeper turned away without a word and started walking back in the direction from where it came.

"Why are you going that way? You turned around," I said in its mind.

It turned its head and called back to me. "If you sssay true, Ender, then thisss desert not sssafe!"

"Good idea, creeper," I replied. *"Be well..."*

Then with a *zip*, I teleported closer to the mountain.

The mountain was tall and imposing, full of shadows and comprised almost entirely of raw, grey stone. In one tall cliff face, a massive cave yawned at the desert and extended into darkness. Other small caves pocketed the stone here and there. Standing in the shadow of an oak tree, I could see the green skin of a zombie moving around inside a small cave nearby, standing just outside the sunlight.

I warped closer.

Watching from the shadows, I saw the zombie standing just inside the dark of the tunnel, frantically hopping from foot to foot, twitching, his hands wringing together. His face was an almost comical expression of fear and suspense.

I approached on foot, and climbed down into the cave to speak with the frightened mob.

Upon seeing my tall and slender form block the sunny sky outside, the zombie seemed terrified. His black eyes opened wide, and a long, whining moan grew from his mouth, open in a silent scream.

"*Easy, zombie,*" I said into his mind. "*Do not fear—I mean you no harm.*"

"What?!" the zombie cried. His voice was thick and dull. "You talk in my head?? Don't hurt me!"

41

"I am Elias. I'm looking for something. Do not be afraid. What is your name?"

"Name?!" the zombie asked. He was still frantic. "What do you want??"

"There is something in this area killing Ender—" I paused. *"Killing mobs. Do you know anything about it?"*

The zombie reached up and grabbed his head. "Yes! Killing! I'm *stuck* in here. Why am I so afraid? I don't know! What am I *doing* here?"

"You ..." I said, *"You have seen something killing mobs?"*

"There's something killing mobs?!" the zombie shrieked. "I mean—yes! There's something killing mobs! Killers in armor with swords! In the *cave!* Why am I here? Why am I so scared??"

The zombie wasn't thinking straight. Maybe zombies' brains were ... funny. I've already seen a zombie burn himself up in the sun the other day, just after we just talked about him hiding from the sunlight. Now seeing this one hiding in the cave, acting like this...

42

"*So you really have seen something,*" I said in his mind. "*Killers in armor … swords? Where did they come from?*"

"Killers in armor?! Where? Oh yeah—the cave! They're in *the cave*. Who?? Why am I so scared? What am I doing down here?"

I considered the situation.

The zombie was totally crazy.

Were the killers some armored Minecraftians who had taken up residence in that huge cave in the side of the stone mountain?

"*Zombie, calm down!*" I said. "*You must have climbed down here to get away from the sunlight, right? Do you mean here? Or the big cave in the side of the mountain?*"

"No … yes! Why would I—?"

He quieted immediately, cocking his head and listening toward the entrance of the cave. I heard it too. Something was moving out there. Footsteps. *Fast* footsteps. The zombie stood, listening, his jaw slack.

43

"Here they come!" he said, then turned to the exit, stuck his arms out in front of him, and started plodding his zombie feet toward the sunlight.

"*Wait!*" I cried out into his mind. "*Don't go out there!*"

I heard their voices, and closed my eyes, reaching out with my *Chi* to feel their minds and understand their words. Two of them. Two *Minecraftians*, I bet ... saying something about ... rabbits.

The shadows of their forms darted past the opening of the cave, blotting out the sun for an instant, and then the zombie was emerging from the entrance after them! He let out a snarl and a moan, then pursued them around the corner into the bright sunlight. Before the zombie was out of sight, I saw him *burst into flames!* He hissed and snarled in pain, but went after the Minecraftians anyway.

I heard the flames, the zombie's pain, and the rapid footsteps return.

"Ha ha ... stupid zombie!" one of them said. I heard them attack the crazy zombie. The undead creature took a few hits, then cried out one last moan, and fell, dead.

The two unseen Minecraftians laughed again, then ran away, continuing into the desert.

Once I couldn't sense their minds near me anymore, I teleported out to the surface, then immediately warped over to the tree line to hide in the shadows. The zombie was gone, of course.

So *that* was it. *Those* were the killers.

There were at least *two Minecraftians* living in the cave in the side of the mountain. They must have moved in, then started doing whatever Minecraftians do, killing all of the mobs in the area while they were at it...

It seemed like a sound theory, but I'd have to watch and gather information, just to be sure. And then, if what I had surmised was indeed the case, it was then my duty to kill them or drive them off to restore the *balance* to this place...

Defeating two armored Minecraftians was a worthy battle. Master would be pleased.

Taking my time and being careful, I teleported in small jumps, closer and closer to the large cave mouth, staying inside the shadows of the mountain. After running by me and killing the zombie, I was sure that the Minecraftians were long gone—off to find rabbits in the desert or whatever they were doing.

But they would be back.

And I would be waiting. Watching, for now...

The mountain was full of outcroppings and jutting areas of rock, huge and grey, full of long, black shadows. It was *perfect* for my ninja approach.

Once I was closer to the huge cave, I saw the twinkling of torchlight deep inside, and as I approached, I eventually settled on a dark shadowy area up above the entrance, where I could stay hidden in the darkness, and watch.

Down below, the mouth of the cave extended into the mountain a bit, before ending in a big stone bowl. It looked like the cave used to continue as a huge tunnel into the mountain, but the tunnel ended in a cobblestone wall, decorated with a central door and a couple of torches.

The Minecraftians had blocked up the tunnel and made it the entrance to their own underground home.

Across the rocky bowl of the cave entrance, in another wall, was *another* door and blocked up tunnel.

So there were two entrances—a larger one and a smaller one—into the unknown underground lair of these killer creatures.

For the rest of the day, I sat in my shadow and meditated, listening for the return of the two Minecraftians. At one point, I pulled the red flower out of my dimensional pocket, and thought about it some more.

Once the sun started going down, I was broken out of my meditation by the sound of footsteps hissing in the sand, and I heard the voices of the two Minecraftians running home while laughing and casually talking about a desert temple.

As they approached, running out of the desert and up the rocky area leading to the cave, I got my first real look at the *Minecraftian race*.

They were both about the size of the zombies I had met—still considerably shorter than I was. They were stocky. Muscular. Both were dressed in clothing, and wore a variety of armor on their bodies and heads. Their skin, unlike the green of the zombies, was vibrant and smooth. They were *living* creatures—not undead. They were fast, and seemed very healthy … and dangerous.

One of the Minecraftians wore a green shirt and blue pants, had short brown hair and a dark beard on his face. He was armored in an iron breastplate and helmet, and wore the skin of animals—leather—on his arms and legs. He carried a metal sword in his hand while he ran.

"Dude, that was awesome!" he said. "I can't *believe* there was one so close!"

48

"Yeah," the other one said, "and there were a lot more openings to the outside than I thought. That would be a surprise if we tried to make a base there!"

The other Minecraftian looked like a brute. His clothing was all black, and he was decked out from head to toe in iron armor, with a shield on one arm, and an iron sword in his other hand.

"LuckyMist, it's almost night!" the green one said. "Are you coming up?"

"Yeah, I was just coming up!" I heard another voice, and then a *third* Minecraftian opened the door of the smaller dwelling. This one was different. Smaller, thinner, a voice that was higher in pitch.

Female.

She stood in the open doorway, dressed in pink and blue, covered with iron armor. I could see that her hair was long and dark under the helmet. In her hand was some sort of tool—a pick axe.

Three Minecraftians.

"How goes the mining?" the fully-armored one asked.

"Pretty quiet, actually," she said, and put her hands on her hips. "You know, WolfBroJake, if you guys didn't run off exploring and killing stuff all the time, and actually *helped* me down there, we'd get more iron!"

She closed the door behind her and stepped into the stone bowl of the cave mouth to join the others.

The big guy shrugged. WolfBroJake. "Sorry, LuckyMist. Blame your *boyfriend*. If Xenocide99 wasn't bugging me so much about checking out the temple he saw," he casually pointed his sword at the other Minecraftian male in the green shirt, "we could build this place up a little faster..."

Okay, I thought. So the female was *LuckyMist*. The big warrior was *WolfBroJake*, and the other male was *Xenocide99*. I wondered if there were any more.

"Oh boy, here they come..." Xenocide99 said.

I heard the plodding footsteps of a zombie walking up the rocky hill to the cave mouth, and heard the clatter of skeleton bones down below.

Xenocide99 stashed his sword and produced a bow, then immediately began firing arrows at the mobs near their cave entrance.

"I'm going inside," LuckyMist said. "Can we go inside and sleep, *please?*"

"Hang on a sec," Xenocide99 said. "We'll be in after we kill these guys."

He continued firing at the mobs. A skeleton returned fire, and Xenocide99 stepped to the side as an arrow flew past, landing in the cobblestone wall next to their cave-home's front door.

From my vantage point, I could see a *small army* of mobs appearing in the desert and surrounding areas, many of whom were suddenly interested in what was going on up here at the cave mouth. Several zombies were slowly converging on the area. There were a few skeletons. I saw the shadow of a creeper. In the

51

distance, I saw the glowing red eyes of spiders appearing, and ...

Zip.

An Enderman appeared, too!

"Enderman!" WolfBroJake exclaimed.

"Whatever," LuckyMist said. She scoffed. "I'm going inside!" And she did, disappearing into the main entrance next to the arrow in the wall.

"I'm on it!" said Xenocide99, and took aim at the Ender with his bow.

I could feel the *Chi* of the non-Order Enderman before he noticed me. I could also feel his energy explode into fury as the Minecraftian took aim with the bow. My fellow Enderman opened his mouth and bared his black teeth, his purple eyes flaring in anger.

There would be no stopping him now.

I did not recognize the Enderman.

"Flee, Brother!" I called out to him in his mind. *"I'm on this—fly! They'll kill you if you stay!"*

The Enderman paused his charge and looked straight up at me in my hiding place for a moment. *"What?!"* he exclaimed in my mind. *"A ninja from the Order? What are you doing here?? I'm going to kill these punks!"*

"Do not fight!" I responded. *"They are Ender killers! Turn and warp away from here!"*

The other Enderman shook his head, ignoring my warning, his jaws open and hungry for satisfaction. He *charged* at the duo, but still spoke to me with his mind voice as he attacked. *"Screw that, brother! I'm going to put these puny creatures in their place. How dare they raise a weapon to me??"*

Xenocide99 finally fired, his aim true, but the Enderman warped out of the way of the shot just before he was hit, and the arrow skittered off harmlessly on the stone hill. Not fazed by his miss, the Minecraftian archer put away his bow and pulled his sword before the Enderman closed the distance.

As the tall, furious Enderman charged at Xenocide99, WolfBroJake sidestepped until he was flanking the attacker, then expertly cut into my fellow Enderman with his sword! The three of them fought for a while—the enraged Enderman and the two Minecraftian warriors—but the Enderman didn't stand a chance. He flailed at them randomly with his powerful fists, but the two armored creatures timed their attacks and worked together to keep him distracted and stunned, until his otherworldly howl cut through the night … and he fell.

Fool, I thought.

I tried to warn him. There was nothing I could do to help. If I had intervened, it would have only blown my cover, and I don't have all of the information of the situation yet. No time to plan. No ability to make a precision strike. I am ninja. I would fight the Minecraftians on my *own* terms, *if* I chose to fight.

The Enderman who just died was defeated before he even began.

His *anger* was his first enemy…

Once the Minecraftians killed the Enderman, I was shocked to see his body dissolve into black smoke and disappear—save for his precious Ender Pearl. It fell from his melting body, hit the stone, and rolled until it stopped at WolfBroJake's feet. He picked up the sacred artifact, and stashed it away into his pack.

I watched for a while as the Minecraftian males proceeded to run around the entrance of their home and the desert nearby, killing all of the mobs they came across, all while laughing and chatting casually about what they were going to do tomorrow.

These Minecraftians had *no regard* for the mob lives. Even the noble Endermen. They killed them, like squishing *bugs*, and laughed about it.

My duty was to keep a balance and protect the neutrality of Overworld.

Minecraftians did have their place in the balance of this world, of course. But *this* place, Nexus 426, was not it. Here, they were an abomination. Obviously they couldn't be reasoned with.

55

So I decided that tomorrow, I would divide them, and eliminate them one at a time…

Day 4 - Overworld

Over the night, I sat up on my perch of darkness and meditated.

The flower.

It was beautiful and delicate, but strong enough to push itself up out of the ground. Was that it? It could be delicate … and be *strong* at the same time?

No.

It had to be something having to do with two different qualities existing at the *same time*. But what was it?

In the morning, the zombies and skeletons burst into flames, and the door to the Minecraftians' main home opened.

The two males, WolfBroJake and Xenocide99, immediately sprang out from inside with swords raised high, and they excitedly pursued the burning undead, trying to land killing blows on the ones that weren't quite dead yet.

LuckyMist walked out from behind them, watched them killing the zombies and skeletons. She sighed, and walked to the other door.

"Guys!" she called out, annoyed. "We should *mine* today! Will you come with me into the mine?"

"Hang on, babe!" Xenocide99 said, running from mob to mob.

"WolfBroJake?" she called. "Would *you* at least help me?"

The big warrior seemed torn, and stood for a while in the sand thinking about it.

"Come on, man, look at all of the loot out in the sand!" Xenocide99 said. "And I thought we were gonna go check out that ravine! We can get some ore *there!*"

LuckyMist crossed her arms in a huff, and went into the mine, slamming the door closed behind her.

She would be my first target. If only I could get through the door…

Suddenly, WolfBroJake ran up to the mine's entrance, and opened the door to go inside, staring back longingly at all of the mob loot floating around in the desert.

This is it, I thought. *That's my chance…*

Looking around the corner of the cave's mouth, I saw a few remaining undead mobs hiding in the shadows of the forest. I broke a small rock off of my ledge where I hid, then threw the stone into the dark woods to create a distraction.

The rock clattered. A zombie moaned.

"Zombie!!" the two Minecraftian males both said in unison.

WolfBroJake abandoned the open door, running down and around to the source of the falling rock, and, joined by his buddy, Xenocide99, they attacked the group of undead mobs in the trees.

When the undead were finished off, Xenocide99 spoke up again.

"Come on, man! Raviiiiinne…"

"Okay, dude," WolfBroJake said. "Let's go check it out, but *just for a sec!* Then we have to come back and help LuckyMist!"

"Awesome!" Xenocide99 exclaimed. "That's a deal!"

And they were off, chasing after mob drops in the desert, then out of sight heading to the supposed ravine.

When all was quiet again, I warped down to the rocky bowl at the cave mouth—the place where they killed the Enderman and several other mobs the night before.

I looked over at the open door to the mine. LuckyMist was down there.

Looking at the closed door to their home, I walked over and looked through the window.

The inside of their *cave house* was lit up by torches, and I could just barely see furniture and tools. Red-colored beds, a table with small tools hanging from it, a stone *forge* of some kind. I reached out with my *Chi* to get a feel for the room's layout. I was sure I'd end up fighting one of them in there later. Maybe the last one. Perhaps if I killed LuckyMist down in the mine, then I could separate the males on the way back from the ravine, and take out the weaker one. Then I could face the last remaining Minecraftian inside the house...

I spun around as I heard a footstep and the scratch of a boot on gravel, and there was LuckyMist, at the entrance to the mine, staring at me. Her eyes were wide and her mouth was open in surprise...

Fool! I thought. I lost my element of surprise! Spent too long looking and planning, without *doing!*

"Ohmygod!!!" she cried, and bolted down the stairs. The door was still open.

I was on her in a second—my long legs and ninja training let me run like the wind. We were in a tunnel of stairs going down, ever down, deep into the world. She looked back over her shoulder, and I saw her eyes grow wide in terror from under her helmet. I was right behind her...

Zip!

Suddenly I warped down the stairs to be in front of her.

She screamed, and turned around to run up the stairs again.

Zip!

I teleported above her again, was waiting while she looked back, and then struck out with a *palm strike* that landed in the middle of her chest plate!

LuckyMist grunted in pain, and fell back, tumbling down the stairs. Amazingly, she found her feet under her and was suddenly running down the long staircase into her mine again.

As I sprinted after her, torches flashed past my face, every seven-or-so stairs.

We reached the bottom of her mine, and she scrambled through the entry room and around a corner into a tunnel. I ran past several chests and furnaces. Turning the corner after her, I saw the

Minecraftian female fleeing down one of her mining tunnels.

Zip!

I warped over to appear in front of her. She screamed in surprise again, screeched to a halt on the stone floor, but didn't react fast enough as I punched her again, then sent a *roundhouse kick* into her midsection. My foot *clanged* against her armor, and she was knocked down onto her back, sliding across the floor.

Wow, these little Minecraftians were *tough* with their armor!

Instead of trying to run away again when she got to her feet, LuckyMist surprised me by instead rapidly building a cobblestone wall to *separate* us—to block me away into her mining tunnel, and leave her safe in the central hub of her mine.

"Ohmygod ohmygod!"

But she wasn't fast enough. I am the warping wind...

Zip!

Just before she completed the defensive wall, I teleported through the hole, past her, and ended my warp just behind her.

LuckyMist turned away from her quickly-built cobblestone shield, and gasped when she found herself cornered. Tall and dark, I stood over her like unstoppable *death*.

I finished her off.

And I was startled when her body suddenly *disappeared* in a puff of smoke!

All of her gear fell to the floor.

I just killed a Minecraftian, I thought. *I could do this!*

The other two would surely put up more of a fight. Dealing with WolfBroJake and Xenocide99 would be more like a battle than a predator chasing prey—but I could handle it. I was certain. I was *ninja*. I'd make my master proud, and I knew that he would grant me the rank of lower ninja when these Minecraftians were destroyed!

I felt confident.

But there wasn't much time. I didn't want to be caught down here for a melee battle. There was practically no room to warp around.

But first...

Looking over the scattered gear that LuckyMist dropped when she died, I observed all of the pieces of her iron armor, multiple pick axes, a metal sword, some other tools, several dozen blocks of cobblestone, some dirt, torches...

As a precaution, I took the pieces of her armor, and put them into my dimensional pocket.

Just in case.

Then I warped my way back up the stairs to the surface.

When I was close to the top of the mine, I could hear the voices of the two males approaching.

Too late!

It was a good thing that I could see my hiding place from inside the stair-tunnel. Taking a chance, I teleported up to my old hiding place … *zip* … and it worked! The two warriors didn't seem to notice my particles flying through the air at light speed.

Below me, the two remaining Minecraftians approached casually, one of them eating the meat of an animal.

"No, man, that was *lame,*" WolfBroJake said. "How did you even think that was a ravine?"

"Well, it was almost dark when I saw it! I guess it was shallower than it looked," Xenocide99 responded.

"I guess your *head* is shallower than it looks," WolfBroJake said, then laughed.

The other male scoffed.

"Guys!" a female voice cried out from inside the house. "Ohmygod you guys are back! *Help me!*"

The door to the house sprung open, and there was LuckyMist! She wasn't wearing her armor, and was dressed in nothing but her pink and blue clothing, but there she was!

Alive!

A small amount of Enderman rage blew up deep inside me, but I *seized* the anger, processed it, and swallowed it back down.

How did that happen? I *killed* her. And I took her stuff! She died right in front of me—by my hand!

"LuckyMist? What happened?" Xenocide99 asked. They ran up to her.

She was frantic. "There was an Enderman in the mine and he *killed* me. This stupid mine! I'm so tired of this place—I want to go *home!*"

"Well how did that happen?" WolfBroJake asked. "Isn't your mine totally safe?"

"Yeah it was!" she said. "Until you left the *door open*, you big dummy!"

"Oops," he said.

67

Xenocide99 laughed. "Uh, sorry, babe. Well, where is it now?"

"Still down there, as far as I know," she said. "And my stuff is going to de-spawn any second!"

"Well let's go down there with you so you can get your stuff," WolfBroJake said.

The three of them ran into the mine and down the stairs.

And they left the *door to the house* open…

Moments later, I was slipping in through the open door, and looking around their very basic cave-home.

I knew that they'd be back any moment, but something was going on with these Minecraftians that I didn't understand, and I would have to improvise.

LuckyMist didn't die.

I killed her, and she came back. But when she *did* come back, it was *here*, in the house…

I searched high and low, reaching out with my *Chi* for anything of power—any artifacts, or items with teleport energy—anything that they might be using to teleport away from their bodies instead of dying. Or maybe … were they coming back to life? Coming back from the dead somewhere else?

Whatever it was, whatever weird magic or technology they were using to resurrect themselves, it was here, somewhere...

The main room was large, and held the crafting table and forge I had already seen, as well as three beds. There was another room off to the side, full of chests. A third room branched off from the opposite side of the main room, but it looked like the third room was still under construction. Well-lit by torches, that room was *empty*, and still had dirt walls...

That's it, I thought. That's what I'd do.

New plan.

I'd hide in the house until night, then kill them all in their sleep!

Dirt. I could work with dirt.

Pulling blocks of dirt out of the wall, as fast as I could before they returned, I carved out a dark space large enough for me to wait in comfortably, then I blocked myself into the wall.

Hidden. Entombed.

Unless the Minecraftians came into the house and decided to continue the excavation of this room, I would be well-hidden until later, when they were all in bed.

It wasn't long before they came back.

The three Minecraftians entered the house loudly, talking and arguing. LuckyMist was angry that she lost her armor, and they didn't have enough iron to make any more. I listened to their conversation, muffled a little by the dirt wall. Sitting in the darkness, I meditated, preparing my mind and body for the mission, letting their words drift across my mind and paint a picture of the Minecraftian way of life. I could imagine the three of them arguing in the main room...

I heard one of them walking into each side room, one at a time, maybe to make sure there were no scary Endermen ninjas hiding inside...

"How about you just make some *leather* armor like mine?" Xenocide99 asked.

"Because, I want my *iron* armor," she responded in a huff. "Besides—we need to save that leather to make books for the enchanting table!"

"Then let's go mine some more and get some more iron!"

"No *way!* I'm not going back in there today! That *thing* could still be in there somewhere. No way I could focus on mining after that!"

There was a pause.

"Besides," she said. "There was something *weird* about that one. Different from the others. Another weird, different mob, like the giant skeleton."

Giant skeleton? I thought. Interesting.

"What the heck *is* that thing, anyway?" WolfBroJake asked. "I've seen every mob there is, and I've never seen a skeleton like *that*. That thing was invincible!"

"What's with all these weird mobs?" LuckyMist said. "I just want to go home, back to our castle, where I can mine and farm and stuff— it's like this world is getting taken over by weird … *mutants* or something."

"What was different about the Enderman?" Xenocide99 asked.

"Uh … well, he was *smart*," LuckyMist said, "and he had some sort of bandana on his head. He wasn't making any noise or was super angry like they get. He was fast, and *sneaky*, and very good with his attacks! He *kicked* me! Can you believe it?"

The two males laughed. "You mean like some sort of Enderman *ninja* or something? Did he throw ninja stars?"

"It's not funny!" LuckyMist cried. "It was … really scary! And he teleported around all … tactical-like!"

"There's definitely something *funny* going on in Diamodia," WolfBroJake said.

"I do agree with LuckyMist about our castle," Xenocide99 said. "It would sure be nice to get it back. I'm all for starting up new bases and starting over and stuff—but that was a *nice place*."

I listened on as they talked for the rest of the day. Sometimes, they left and came back—at least the males did. I was pretty sure that LuckyMist stayed in the house for the rest of the afternoon.

Every once and a while, I smelled different scents coming from their furnace, Overworld smells that I couldn't identify. She must have been making some Minecraftian *food*.

When night came around, I heard the males fighting outside—it was probably a regular thing for them to kill the mobs that came to their door when the sun went down.

Eventually, they were all inside.

Once the talking died down, I reached out with my *Chi*, and felt for their minds, felt for their energy...

These Minecraftians had *huge* energy. They were so full of *purpose*, even just in the moment, if they were a little aimless with direction. They were, to be sure, some of the strongest beings in this universe. And I had a feeling that these were just *typical* Minecraftians—not the paragons of their race, not the leaders. Not the *masters*.

When their energy calmed down, I decided to wait another hour, then silently removed the dirt blocks from my concealment wall.

I stepped out.

Moving with precise and silent steps, I first checked the reflections of everything on the nearest wall of the main room for any subtle movements around the corner, then carefully looked with my own eyes.

The three Minecraftians were laying down, sleeping, each on a separate red bed.

Endermen don't sleep, so I didn't fully understand sleep at the time. Looking back on it now, I realize that I didn't have to be quite as cautious as I was, but I don't regret my careful planning and movements. I am ninja. Stealth can *never* be overdone.

Seeing all three of those Minecraftians lying in their beds with their eyes closed—I assumed that they were meditating. I thought that they'd be aware of me once I was in the room, so I made plans to move as quickly and as efficiently as possible once I sprang into action...

Closing my eyes, I mentally prepared myself for the intense focus needed to attack *all three* of them, while also solving the problem of the Minecraftians coming back to life on the fly...

There were *two* torches in the room. One in the front by the door, and one in the back by the beds.

My master's voice drifted through my head.

"We must not learn to try harder. The key is to learn how not to try in the first place..."

I *knew* what I had to do. I would trust in my instincts to guide me.

I would not try.

I would do…

Suddenly taking great, silent leaps across the room from the hall, I near-instantly punched and destroyed the two torches, plunging the room into total darkness.

In that second, the Minecraftians still hadn't reacted, so I moved onto *phase two*, and immediately set myself onto WolfBroJake, the strongest fighter, and punched him again and again, with all of my *Chi* behind my attacks, to take him out first! My strong fists, as black as ink, pounded into his armored form again and again. He grunted, and barely started to struggle, then died…

WolfBroJake disappeared in a puff of smoke, his armor, shield, sword, and all of his other gear falling on the bed and scattering out across on the floor.

Phase three.

In the next instant, I was attacking Xenocide99. My fists moved like dark lightning, and he managed to jump out of his bed after taking several hits.

"What the—what's happening?!" he cried, his eyes wide in the darkness.

LuckyMist screamed and jumped out of bed, but in the dark, she hit the wall, and didn't know where to go. The female pulled out her pickaxe as I pummeled Xenocide99. The remaining male grunted under the assault, and pulled his sword, trying to back away but getting stuck on the bed.

I could see his confused and terrified expressions in purple light of my fierce, glowing eyes.

Suddenly, in the corner of my eye, I saw the white shape of WolfBroJake's pale face appearing again in the dark. He was standing on his bed, armor-less, dressed only in his black clothes with nothing in his hands...

"What's going on?!" WolfBroJake cried.

It was the beds!

Their *beds* were the source of their regeneration!

Before they realized my intentions, I pushed Xenocide99's armored chest with a mighty palm strike, and he fell backwards over his bed. That would give me a few moments.

WolfBroJake took just a single step off of the bed before I was on him again. Without his sword and armor, he was *nothing* next to my martial arts skill, and died again after a few well-placed hits. As soon as his body disappeared into a puff of smoke again, my next movement was a powerful block-breaking move. I let out a roaring *kiai*, a shout to focus my *Chi* into the attack, and my elbow *exploded* into WolfBroJake's bed, smashing it into a thousand pieces!

LuckyMist screamed, and Xenocide99 dropped his sword in fear.

WolfBroJake did not come back. I don't know where he'd reappear, *if* he'd reappear, but it wouldn't be in *here*.

For the moment, I ignored the wounded Xenocide99 and the terrified LuckyMist, and I moved to destroy the remaining male's bed. Xenocide99 seemed to realize what I was doing, and he reached for his sword in the dark. I rapidly kicked the Minecraftian weapon out of his reach, as I set up to perform another breaking move on the bed.

I roared another *kiai*, and struck down with my elbow, sundering the bed into pieces of wood and wool!

"It's the Enderman!" Xenocide99 cried. "He's breaking our beds!"

"Where's WolfBroJake??" LuckyMist screamed.

Xenocide99 jumped to his feet and pulled his bow, backing into the open front area of the main room. Being so dark, I can only assume that he was aiming for my glowing eyes.

Zip!

I saw it coming, so it was easy to warp out of the way. I looked down to LuckyMist, who still had her back to the wall.

Thunk!

In a sudden splash of *pain*, I realized that I wasn't paying attention, and Xenocide99 managed to fire off a second arrow faster than I anticipated. His arrow stuck out of my side...

The Enderman rage boiled up inside of me, and I fought to push it back down.

My eyes must have flared, and I was sure that I looked terrifying to him, because he turned white with fear, and fumbled to nock another arrow.

Torchlight suddenly appeared in the room. LuckyMist must have thrown a torch up on one of the walls. Risking a quick glimpse, I saw her rooting around through WolfBroJake's items cast around on the floor.

Xenocide99 fired at me again, but I was ready.

Zip!

I warped behind him, and beat on him with fists and palm strikes until he died in a puff of smoke! His iron and leather armor, bow and arrows, and other items fell and scattered on the stone floor.

Zip!

Teleporting onto LuckyMist's bed, I reached into the air, winding up for another *breaking strike*, then roared and smashed the bed apart!

I would finish this. I would be victorious.

The threat to Nexus 426 was almost neutralized.

Turning to face LuckyMist for our second battle, I saw what she was trying to find in WolfBroJake's items. She held his *shield* in front of her, cowering behind it.

"Ohmygod ohmygod! What am I gonna do???" she cried.

I approached. I almost didn't have the heart to kill her…

81

But the mission came first.

Balance must be restored.

Like lightning, I attacked with multiple palm strikes, each hitting the shield. The *thunk* of my palm hitting the wood and iron made LuckyMist shudder in fear, and as my assault continued, and the shield began to splinter, she babbled on and on, pleading for me to stop.

"We'll leave! We'll go! Please stop! Is that what you want?? We'll leave!!"

I paused.

I could hear her out, at least.

Without the others, she was mostly harmless, and I could kill her at will.

Without warning, I stopped my attack, and immediately sat into a meditation pose on the stone floor, surrounded by a mess of Minecraftian items.

The silence in the room was surprising...

LuckyMist stood holding the shield above her, like she was when I was pounding on it, whimpering, breathing hard, until she finally peeked over the edge of her defense out of curiosity...

"I am calling a temporary truce to hear what you have to say, LuckyMist," I said, speaking into her mind.

Shocked, she dropped the shield with a loud *clang* and grabbed her head with her hands.

"What?!" she cried. "What did you say?? Did you ... *say something* ... in my *head?* Was that in my head?"

"Where are the others?" I asked with the mind voice. *"Where are they right now?"*

"OMG, you *are* in my head! Please don't hurt me! I mean you no harm!"

"Where are the others, LuckyMist?" I repeated.

"Okay ... you ... can talk in my head. Okay. *Them?"* She paused, shocked, thinking, confused.

"Oh, uh … with their … *beds* gone, they could be anywhere! They're far away. Ohmygod, they're far away, and it's the middle of the night!"

"They are reborn, but elsewhere?"

"Um … yeah. Without … without the beds," she gestured at the devastation around the room— the pieces of wood and wool and items scattered all over, "they'll respawn somewhere near … near the castle … ohmygod …" She suddenly looked terrified, thinking of something frightening, then she looked up at me. "Are you going to kill me again? Please don't kill me again! It's night time!"

"Tell me about this castle." I said. *"Tell me about the giant skeleton…"*

Day 5 – Overworld

Over the rest of the night and into the morning, I talked with LuckyMist.

She told me about their story as she picked up and organized all of the dropped items and cleaned up the broken beds.

My investigation of the Enderman deaths at Nexus 426 revealed this trio of Minecraftians, but *they* were just a symptom of a *larger* upset in the balance of the world...

Like I mentioned before, this world has a *place* for Minecraftians. As the natural opposition to the mobs, there will always be battle wherever they go. But they tend to settle, and ultimately, an area becomes better off because of the Minecraftian presence.

My master must have sensed the disturbance along with the tragedy of the Endermen deaths, because otherwise, he would have seen wisdom in allowing the Minecraftians to stay *here*, in this cave, to make a new home, to get settled and establish a balance over time.

But something was wrong.

These Minecraftians were displaced from their own home by an abomination. Something I'd never heard of before, either in my teachings from my master, or on my Seed Stride.

She told me the story about a 'Skeleton King' who attacked the Minecraftians in their own castle—a gigantic skeleton with thick bones, wearing armor and wielding a huge, *different* kind of bow. An intelligent skeleton who spoke in a booming, menacing voice, and had red glowing eyes.

And not only was this *Skeleton King* immensely powerful on his own terms—he also led a skeleton army who followed his orders and worked well together.

My mission to restore balance had grown more complicated than merely neutralizing some Minecraftians...

It seemed that a true abomination may be involved.

I would have to investigate this.

LuckyMist and I made a deal. She was also speaking for Xenocide99 and WolfBroJake, but assumed that they'd be all for it.

The Minecraftians would abandon their cave home here next to Nexus 426. That would solve the problem of the Endermen deaths. In return, I would travel with them to their castle to the east, and help them get their home back.

My new mission was to restore the balance in this part of Overworld by destroying the Skeleton King and scattering his skeleton army.

Over the course of the day, I meditated and focused on healing the arrow wound I had incurred in the battle. I hoped that through my continued experience, I would finally master the art of the *Chi dodge*, and be able to dodge arrows on instinct like all mature Endermen do.

LuckyMist prepared the cave home to be broken down, to take all of their furniture, gear, and belongings with us back to the castle. She mentioned that there was a village on the way, and hoped that they could leave all of their things *there* until the castle was safe again.

I hadn't seen a *village* yet on my Seed Stride...

Xenocide99 and WolfBroJake eventually made their way back to the cave home, together. After a surprised and tense moment when they realized that the Enderman ninja was still in their home, LuckyMist related the entire story to them. Even though the two males were very *wary* of me, they were onboard with the idea.

"And here," I said to LuckyMist in her mind. *"This belongs to you..."*

I produced all of her armor from my dimensional pocket, and gave them to her, piece by piece.

"My armor!" she exclaimed, grinning ear to ear. "No wonder we couldn't find it!"

"You are *some kind* of Enderman," Xenocide99 said. WolfBroJake nodded.

As the three Minecraftians packed up all of their gear, and recovered the resources and furnaces stored in the mine, I sat in the rocky bowl of the cave entrance, my legs crossed, holding the red flower before me.

The flower was strong, because it pushed up out of the ground. It was beautiful, and a symbol of hope, because it thrived against adversity.

I had given up on some sort of lesson about *duality*.

Was it really so *simple* that it was strong and beautiful, even though it had to push itself up out of the mud and dirt?

"Oh, what's with the flower?"

LuckyMist walked up behind me.

"My master gave it to me to contemplate. There is a lesson in the flower."

"Oh, really?" she said. "I'm really familiar with those red ones. I've got a whole flowerbed full of them back at the castle. Well … if they're still there, that is."

"Something beautiful, but also fleeting," I said. *"Maybe … even though it's strong and beautiful, it's still only here for a moment."*

"I dunno," she said. "There's something really interesting about those."

"What's that?" I asked in her mind.

"Well, when they grow, they need a lot of *dirt* under them so that they can push through long, strong roots. If they don't, they'll just be a boring plant. But if they can get those long roots all the way through that tough dirt and mud, then they can finally make the pretty red flowers."

"So … it's not beautiful despite the dirt. It's beautiful because it has to push through the dirt. It needs to push through the dirt to become beautiful…"

"Yeah, maybe," she said.

I paused, and let the revelation roll over me. My *Chi*, the pearl in my center felt warm…

"*Thank you, flower,*" I said, then I handed the pretty red plant to LuckyMist.

"For me?" she said, taken aback.

I nodded.

She took the flower and smiled. "Thanks!" Then she walked away.

Soon after, the Minecraftians were ready to travel. We would stay in the cave home overnight, and then set off in the morning to the village on the way to the castle.

We were off to fight the Skeleton King…

Box Set Book 2:
Diary of an Enderman Ninja

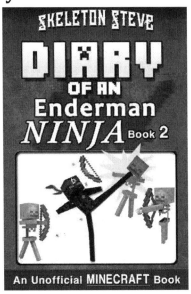

They're off to kill the Skeleton King!

After Elias the Enderman Ninja discovered the source of the Endermen murders near Nexus 426, he learned that the Minecraftians' presence was a symptom of an even bigger problem--the Skeleton King and his army of skeleton archers! Will a temporary alliance between the Enderman and the Minecraftians be enough to take down the warlord abomination and restore balance to the area? And will Elias even be able to fight the giant skeleton boss without having completed his ninja training?

Day 6 – Overworld

The sun rose in the eastern sky as the moon set in the west.

I sat, my long legs crossed under me, my powerful Ender hands soft and receptive on my knees, listening to morning on *Overworld*.

My pearl was warm, and I could feel my *Chi* moving in and out of me like waves, brushing up against the *Chi* of the world around me—the hidden *seeds* of Ender Pearls hiding in the dirt surrounding my meditation.

As this strange, vibrant world woke around me, the colors changed from blue to silver, the greens of the forest brightened under the rising sun, and the desert sand blazed like fire stretching out as far as I could see away from me … away from the mountain.

Even though the light hurt my eyes, I couldn't help but admire the living spirit of the Overworld.

The End was my home—simple, dim, devoid of most colors, other than shades of purple and the muted sandy color of the end stone. That, and the *lack* of color that existed behind the swirling and bespeckled purple mist, layer upon layer, of the great, expansive void...

In the quiet of the morning, I watched the zombies and skeletons wander around out in the sand.

The mobs of this world were part of the *balance*.

There was balance in all things. That's why I was here—to correct the *upset* in the balance.

The mobs balanced the Minecraftians, and the Minecraftians balanced the mobs.

When I arrived here at *Nexus 426*, I was sure that I would have to kill the three Minecraftians, the living, striving creatures that were still sleeping in the crude home cut into the mountain behind me. But it turned out that their presence, and the resulting murders of my Ender people in this area, were altogether just a *symptom* of a larger problem with the balance.

Soon, I, an Enderman Ninja, would be traveling with these three ambitious and resourceful Minecraftians to their home far to the south to fight an abomination and help them reclaim their home.

The balance must be restored.

I closed my eyes, sitting straight in my meditation posture, and felt my *Chi* rolling over my body in waves...

I felt powerful, and knew that I would succeed.

I am ninja. I am the warping wind...

This would surely be quite a battle. But Xenocide99 and WolfBroJake were strong fighters in their own right, and LuckyMist was very clever.

An army of skeleton archers?

Finally, I would have to master the *Chi Dodge* if I was to be victorious. My hands and feet

97

and skill in martial arts would scatter the undead to the winds like the bones they are...

My hand went to the wound in my left side, and felt the tender injury from Xenocide99's arrow. By now, I had been focusing my *Chi* in meditation yesterday and over the night while the Minecraftians slept, and the wound was almost healed. But I felt that I would always remember...

The first time I was wounded from an arrow in battle would be a reminder to *stay focused*.

Or, perhaps, I took the wound because I was too focused.

Trying, instead of just doing. Thinking instead of *being*...

I would have to contemplate this. Something inside that riddle would hold the *key* to learning the *Chi Dodge*—I knew it.

As the sun rose higher above the tops of the forest trees, the sky turned bright blue, and the undead roaming the desert burst into flames. Small, walking pillars of fire moved through the sand for several steps before falling, reduced to nothing but smoke, ash, bones, and charred meat.

With my *Chi* attuned to the world around me, I suddenly detected movement and signs of life stirring behind me in the mountain.

And the quiet of the morning was broken.

"Who has the food? I didn't get any food!" Xenocide99 said.

The door to the Minecraftians' cave home popped open, and WolfBroJake stepped out, dressed in his armor, his shield on his arm. The Minecraftian defensive tool was still damaged from my attack on the three of them the night before last.

"I have it," LuckyMist's voice said from inside the improvised house. "Here ya go."

I heard the sound of one of them crunching on the burnt body of an animal.

"Seriously?" LuckyMist said. "You don't have any food?"

"Hey," Xenocide99 responded between bites, "I dropped all of my stuff when that psycho Enderman *killed* me, remember?"

WolfBroJake stepped up next to me. I could sense the uneasiness in his mind as he looked at my meditating form. I could feel his fear and his eyes on me, even though my own eyes were closed.

"*Good morning*," I said to him into his mind. Then I opened my eyes, and stood, towering over the armored warrior.

"Uh … hi," he said aloud, then walked back to the others. "Sun's up, you two. We should get moving."

"Have we got everything?" Xenocide99 asked. "Anything left in the mine?"

"Nothing down there," LuckyMist said.

The two of them stepped out into the sunshine. LuckyMist was wearing her armor again.

I was frequently reminded of how colorful this world was compared to back home. The

Minecraftians' colors were brilliant—Xenocide99 with his bright green shirt and mix of iron and leather armor, LuckyMist's pink shirt standing out under her iron armor. Even the contrast of WolfBroJake's iron armor on his all black clothing was stunning to my Ender eyes.

"Who's carrying doors?" Xenocide99 asked, pulling out his axe and eying the front door of their cleaned-out home. "I'm almost full."

"Me too," LuckyMist said. "I've got all of the food and mining stuff."

"I'm almost full too," WolfBroJake said. "Screw it. Just leave 'em. We can make more."

Xenocide99 shrugged, and put his axe away. The three of them walked over to where I was standing.

"*Lead the way*," I said into their minds. "*I presume you all remember how to return home?*"

Xenocide99 shook his head. "Jeez," he said. "I don't know if I'll *ever* get used to that…"

"It's like I'm thinking thoughts in another voice," LuckyMist said. "So *weird*..."

After a bit more conversation, we began the journey back to the Minecraftians' castle where the Skeleton King and his army sat, upsetting the balance of Overworld.

I decided to be courteous and *walk* with the three creatures, even though I could travel twenty times faster by warping in small jumps across the landscape.

We started by heading to the east into the forest, until we had navigated around the massive stone mountain and were traveling south again. Behind the mountain was a great, green valley full of animals. One side of the valley was bordered with a *different* sort of forest showing white-barked, shorter trees, and the other side of the valley rose in elevation until the ground broke up into canyons, and extreme and jagged hills that dotted the landscape.

As we walked together as a group, I noticed that the two males were following the lead of LuckyMist. Taking a closer look, I saw that she held a small, shiny object in her hand. It was metal, and shaped like a flattened Ender Pearl, with a moving mechanism of Minecraftian technology within.

"*What is that, LuckyMist?*" I asked in her mind.

She was startled out of her concentration, and looked up at me. I noticed, in the sunshine, that her eyes were green. I was reminded of my Master Ee'Char, with his glowing green eyes of the Ender race's most ancient people. LuckyMist's green eyes didn't *glow*, of course.

"Oh, this?" She said, holding the object up so that I could see it better. "This is a *compass*. It's for telling direction. Figuring out which way we're going and where to go next." She held it out to me. "Wanna see?"

I bowed slightly, and took the small metallic object into my long, black hand.

The contraption was carefully crafted out of refined iron ore, with a fine needle and other red material I didn't recognize making up the mechanism in the center. It was remarkable how the Minecraftians could harvest pieces of the Overworld and convert their natural resources into tools and technology to meet their needs. Weapons. Armor. Tools ... things like *this*.

Bending down, I placed the compass back into her hand. She smiled up at me, and checked the compass against the horizon in the direction we were walking again.

Before we reached the end of the valley, Xenocide99 and WolfBroJake drew their metal swords and ran off to attack several cows that were eating the grass nearby. The two Minecraftian males laughed and chatted as they ran from beast to beast, cutting each of them down and collecting their meat and skins. They slaughtered the entire group of cows.

When they returned to our path, they gave the meat to LuckyMist, and she added it to the group's food supply.

"How do beds work?" I asked, as we walked on.

Immediately, my extended *Chi* picked up on the unease of WolfBroJake and Xenocide99 at the question. They tensed, and I could sense them looking at each other with concern as they walked behind me.

"What do you mean?" asked LuckyMist. "They're for *sleeping*."

"They are the source of your ability to be reborn, are they not?"

Xenocide99 spoke up. "Um … not *exactly*," he said. "Where we put down beds is where we *spawn*."

"Spawn?" I asked. *"How is it that you spawn when you are killed?"*

"It's just …" WolfBroJake began. "It's just what we *do*."

"You spawned on your beds when you were killed," I said. *"But when I destroyed your beds, you still spawned—only elsewhere…"*

"*Eh* … can we talk about something else?" Xenocide99 asked.

"Do Minecraftians die?" I asked.

"I guess, when you talk about it like that," LuckyMist said, "I guess we don't. We just *respawn*."

We walked in silence for a while.

"Do you need to … respawn … often?" I asked.

They all scoffed.

"No!" LuckyMist said. "We try *not to*, you know?"

"It's not like we *like dying*, Enderman," WolfBroJake said, his tone sharp.

Xenocide99 stayed quiet for a while. They were all obviously quite uncomfortable. "What about you, ninja? Do *you* respawn when you die?" he asked. His tone was annoyed.

"I do not," I responded. *"Not that I know of. When we Endermen are killed and separated from our Chi, we are gone forever, leaving nothing but our Pearl. Much like what you saw with the Ender you killed the other day..."*

"Okay!" LuckyMist said, her voice giddy. "Let's talk about something else other than *dying*, huh? We're all going to fight the Skeleton King—I'd rather not think about it, okay??"

We walked on, continuing along the path of LuckyMist's compass, through a hilly environment occasionally broken up by forest, until the sun started going down in the western sky, and the Minecraftians started talking about building a temporary shelter.

When the sky started changing color, the three Minecraftians stopped and started building a small *hut* out of dirt blocks up against the tree line of a grassy plain. They built up walls and a crude roof, quickly and with little effort, all using the dirt they had stored on their person. As they milled around, decorating the hut with torches, chopping down some nearby trees, and constructing a furnace out of stone, I warped rapidly around the immediate area, seeking dirt blocks that held pearl seeds.

Here and there, just like all over this world, I could feel out to my surroundings with my *Chi*, and sense the promise of a seed, like a tiny pinprick of light in darkness. Moving my hands, receptive to the energy hidden in the blocks, I drew closer and closer to each seed, then lifted and moved blocks of dirt until I found what I was looking for.

By the time the sun went down, I had placed *five seed blocks* into my dimensional pocket.

Even though my *Seed Stride* was on hold while I was tending to this special mission, I felt that I may as well tend to gathering seeds when I had nothing better to do.

"See?" Xenocide99 said. "We should have brought the *doors*."

"How can we be so full of stuff from the cave house and be so low on resources?" WolfBroJake asked.

"I have mostly mob stuff," Xenocide99 said. "And my gear."

"And I have mostly the tools and mining stuff, what little food we had, and iron … *not much* iron, really!" LuckyMist said. She looked up at me. "That place wasn't fun to live in at all, you know…"

"No big deal I guess," WolfBroJake said. "We can always cut down more trees."

The warrior suddenly put down a crafting table, and built some doors.

"*What problem did you have living in the cave?*" I asked LuckyMist in her mind.

"Oh … everything just kept *going wrong!*" she said. "We lost a lot of stuff when we had to run away from the castle. Hopefully it's all still there. And I spent *days* in the mine, but never found any diamonds, and found barely enough iron to keep replacing my tools…"

When the sky turned silver, then dark, and the mobs started coming out, the three Minecraftians settled inside for the night. WolfBroJake installed a wooden door onto the dirt hut.

"Um," LuckyMist said to me, pausing and turning before going inside, "we didn't make it *tall* enough for you, Elias. Sorry—didn't think about that."

"*Not a problem*," I responded. "*I do not sleep. I will stay out here and keep watch.*"

The two males went inside.

"Well, good night!" LuckyMist said to me.

I bowed slightly, and she turned and went inside, closing the door behind her.

Looking up, I watched the stars for a while as the night cooled, and thought of the void back in *The End*.

After a while, when I sensed that the three Minecraftians were asleep, I teleported up onto the roof of their dirt structure, and settled in to meditate for the night.

Day 7 – Overworld

After an uneventful night, I stood and warped back to the grassy ground when I sensed movement inside the dirt hut.

As the sky brightened with the morning sun, and the undead in the area burned up in the light, the door to the hut opened with a *pop*, and the three Minecraftians sprang out into the open.

"I'm hungry!" Xenocide99 said. "Did you cook those steaks?" he asked LuckyMist as she emerged into the daylight.

"You don't remember? You were there..." she responded flatly.

WolfBroJake walked off a short distance on his own, then started collecting the pieces of the burnt-up undead that were in the grass around their small dwelling.

I observed that LuckyMist and Xenocide99 had an interesting dynamic. The two were clearly *close*, and touched each other frequently, but also bickered a lot. They called each other names other than their own—baby, babe, honey—and treated each other differently than they treated WolfBroJake.

As the three Minecraftians readied themselves, chatting and going over their gear, eating, preparing to continue our journey, I watched them quietly.

Before we left, I pulled one of the dirt blocks out of the corner of their structure, now that the hut had served its purpose and was no longer needed. I could feel the energy of a *pearl seed* reaching out to me from inside of it, so I slipped the block into my dimensional pocket.

WolfBroJake laughed. "Freaking Endermen and their dirt blocks..." he said.

I didn't understand what he meant, and I didn't feel like pursuing his meaning, so I said nothing.

We moved on.

Later, as we walked, the Minecraftians were talking about their food supply, or *lack* of it.

"How can you have so much food and not have any meat?" Xenocide99 said. "You said you had all of the *food stuff*."

"Well, it's mostly ingredients," LuckyMist responded. "You can't eat sugarcane and mushrooms, doofus! Would you like a *beetroot?*"

She pulled a red chunky sphere from her bag and held it in front of Xenocide99's face. He scrunched up his nose in disgust.

"What *do* we have?" WolfBroJake asked.

"Um," LuckyMist said, "We have a little *chicken* left. I can make some bread from this wheat, I guess. I have a few raw potatoes I can cook... It's a good thing you guys killed those cows!"

"We'll find more crops at the village," Xenocide99 said. "I hope that Skeleton King *jerk* hasn't eaten up all of the food we have back home!"

"Yeah, Jeez," LuckyMist said. "We have *so much* food back at the castle." She looked up at me as we walked.

Over the last few days, I'd noticed that LuckyMist was the only Minecraftian among the three of them that ever looked me *in the eyes*.

"We had to abandon so much food back there…" she said to me.

"*Describe the … food back there*," I said.

"Well," she said, "There's *loads* of potatoes, carrots, wheat, beetroot, and other crops down at the farm, and—"

"*Farm?*" I asked. "*What is a farm?*"

"Wow, okay," she said, "Well, it's like … a big open *space* where we grow plants for food! There are chests inside the fence where I was keeping all of the crops and seeds."

"And there's also the *kitchen*," WolfBroJake said. "We have tons of *meat* in there."

"Yeah," LuckyMist responded. "We have a lot of cooked food in the kitchen. And as far as *farms* go, you'll see what they look like when we get to the village. The villagers have farms…"

"We'll be fine if we take our time and don't run," Xenocide99 told them. "We can cook bread and steaks and get more crops and food at the village."

Time passed as we traveled, and the sun moved across the sky.

Eventually, amidst the Minecraftians saying *'we'd be there soon'* and *'it's right around the corner'* a few times, we finally came across the village.

I welcomed a new sight in my exploration of the Overworld as the trees parted, and we walked out into a large, yellowish grassy plain. In the middle of the open area was a collection of a dozen or so structures made of wood and stone. Thin, cobblestone roads ran between the many buildings, and I saw creatures *similar* to the Minecraftians—at least as seen from a distance—bustling around the houses. The late afternoon sunlight cast a golden light over the village and its surrounding field.

It was getting late.

"There it is!" Xenocide99 exclaimed, and ran across the plain. The other two followed him.

I held back and watched.

Would the villagers be hostile toward an Enderman?

Minecraftians certainly were...

I could already tell, as I observed the movement of the creatures from a distance, that the villagers were *different* from the Minecraftians. But, if the Minecraftians looked upon them as allies, then villagers were probably opposed to the mobs.

And that included me.

"*LuckyMist*," I said, using my *mind voice* across the distance.

I saw her stop, halfway between me and the village, as her friends ran on. She turned, and began running back to me.

I warped the rest of the distance between us.

Zip.

She stopped, startled. *"Ohmygod*, that scared me!" She laughed once, then looked away. "Last time you did that … um … *sorry…"*

I felt as though I should show some empathy for her fear—for her *memory* of when I attacked her in the mine. That's clearly what she was thinking about. But as a member of the *Order of the Warping Fist*, I've spent my entire life learning how to control my naturally fierce Ender emotions. So in that moment, I couldn't think of anything comforting to say.

"The villagers," I said into her mind. *"They will be hostile toward me, won't they?"*

She thought for a moment. "Not really." LuckyMist was quiet for a moment, then spoke up again. "You know what? I honestly *don't know!* But if they don't like you, it's not like there's anything they can *do* about it. They'll just keep away from you, I guess…"

I nodded, and we began walking to the village.

In the distance, I could see Xenocide99 and WolfBroJake running around the outskirts of the village, inspecting various shallow structures of dirt surrounded with blocks of wood. Reaching out with my *Chi* to sense their energy, and the energy of the village, I could feel tension in the Minecraftians. The energy of the villagers was strange and hard to interpret, but was mostly a sense of … directionless … *urgency*.

As we approached, Xenocide99 ran up to us. WolfBroJake wasn't far behind.

"There's *nothing!*" Xenocide99 said. "The farms are empty! What the heck?!"

"Just sprouts," WolfBroJake said. "Like they all harvested them recently."

"But villagers never *have* empty farms!" Xenocide99 said. "What are we going to do for food??"

WolfBroJake smirked at his buddy. "Don't freak out, man. We'll figure something out. We'll go hunting or something!"

"Besides," LuckyMist said. "We'll be home soon, and we have all that food back there!"

"If the Skeleton King and his army doesn't *eat* it all," WolfBroJake said.

"Are you kidding?" LuckyMist responded. "They're all undead!"

"Oh yeah," WolfBroJake said, hitting his helmet with his gauntleted hand. *Clank.*

"*If* we can kill a giant intelligent skeleton and an army of skeleton archers," Xenocide99 said. "That's a big *if*..."

None of them talked for a while, and I followed them as they walked into the village, weaving through the streets. I looked at what Xenocide99 had referred to as the 'farms'—several raised plots of tilled soil, surrounded with wooden logs to keep the dirt in, with furrows of water cutting through them. The dark soil was mostly empty, showing only tiny, youngling plants popping out of the ground.

LuckyMist was right about the villagers not being hostile. They were *certainly* afraid of me. As I

119

walked between the small dwellings, the strange villager creatures stared at me with intense, green eyes, furrowed their brows in disapproval, and pressed their lips together, hurrying away from us when they noticed me. The creatures all kept their hands together under their clothes, and darted away to congregate in small groups, staring after me, squawking in their weird language.

"Hurr … Hmm … Hurrrr…."

"Here's the blacksmith!" Xenocide99 said. We all approached a building that was a little different than the others. Under a roofed pavilion, there was a contained forge full of burning lava, and a couple of stone furnaces. A villager dressed in brown and black awkwardly stepped out of the way as Xenocide99 forced his way past him into a small living space.

I heard the Minecraftian creak open a storage chest inside.

"Oh maaaan," Xenocide99 whined. "Just a saddle and an apple. Anyone mind if I eat this apple?"

The others shrugged. "No," they said.

Xenocide99 emerged from inside, pushing his way past the blacksmith again, chomping down on a round, red fruit from a tree.

"Here's one of those bigger houses," WolfBroJake said, pointing at a stone structure just down the street. "We can set up chests and all of our stuff in there. Make a temporary base for attacking the castle!"

"Good idea," LuckyMist said. The three of them moved toward the house, and WolfBroJake opened the door and stepped inside. I followed to the doorway, stooping to look through a window at the building's interior.

In the pink light of the setting sun, I looked at the structure they were interested in. It was a large house, practically empty, with plenty of space and an "L" shaped floorplan. The ceilings were vaulted, and a single torch lit up the inside. As I stood outside looking in, the three Minecraftians sprang into action, placing more torches up high, and lining the walls with wooden chests.

WolfBroJake placed his crafting table in the center of the main room.

I thought back to their battles with the various mobs outside of their cave home.

These Minecraftians were exceptionally skilled in battle. I needed to use considerable strategy, craftiness, and improvised fighting skills to defeat them before. However, they were very *impulsive* when fighting, and were quick to action.

I recalled my master's words, "*The ultimate ninja does not rely on his hands or feet to defeat the opponent, but rather, his mind...*"

If these three were under the impression that, with my aid, we could just charge up to the castle and destroy the Skeleton King and his army, then we could very well *lose* to their lack of thought and planning.

I was a ninja. I would craft a *precision strike*.

Just as I divided these Minecraftians to fight them before—using darkness against them, employing the element of surprise, completely *overwhelming* them—I would insist on doing the same to a skeleton army.

And I had *no doubt* that I would succeed. I was a skilled martial artist and a master of the shadows! I could defeat a mere group of skeletons and whatever passed for their leader. I was Ender. I was *Order of the Warping Fist*…

However, I knew that I could not rely on the Minecraftians to be *patient* when we approached the castle for the first time. LuckyMist could probably be patient, but not the two males. They could not be patient like *I was*, when I watched them and observed their weaknesses before I planned to strike.

I would have to see the castle for myself first.

Alone.

"*Minecraftians*," I said into their minds through the wall of the house.

They stopped their bustling, organizing, and rearranging and looked at me. The males averted their eyes.

123

"Yes?" Xenocide99 asked.

"What is it, Elias?" LuckyMist said.

"You should stay in the village to set up our 'temporary base' and kill animals for food. I would like to go ahead, alone, to examine the castle and the Skeleton Kind from hiding. I will return after I've had a look at where we will have our battle..."

"By yourself?" Xenocide99 said.

"Don't you want us to come? We'll be stronger *together!*" WolfBroJake said.

"Do not worry, Minecraftians," I responded. *"I will not engage the enemy. I will merely observe them and return..."*

"Are you sure?" LuckyMist asked. "It's still pretty far. And, seriously, that army is *really* dangerous..."

"Distance is not a problem, LuckyMist," I said. *"I can travel far faster when I am not walking. I only need to know the way..."*

The three of them looked at each other with concern. I *sensed* their energy, and had a pretty good idea what they were thinking. The Minecraftians held a lot of confidence in my assistance and martial skills being the *key* to them defeating the Skeleton King and reclaiming their home. If something bad happened to me, then they would be without direction, without a home, and without a warrior capable of defeating their enemy...

"Will you at least wait until morning?" LuckyMist said.

I could do that. I would be happy to observe the village and watch how the defense of the town fares over the night against the exploring undead that always come out when the sun goes down.

I'd watch over the Minecraftians.

After placing torches above the doors of all of the village's buildings and lighting up the streets some more, the three of them settled into their new house for the night. I was amused when the villagers all rushed for the safety of their homes by the time the moon came out. Doors slammed closed all around me, and the energy I detected with my *Chi* from the village was that of *fear*...

Day 8 – Overworld

The night was interesting, but uneventful for the most part. Zombies *did* make their way into town, and undead did wander the streets for a while banging on villagers' doors, but they weren't strong enough to break down the town's defenses. The Minecraftians never stepped outside of their home to fight the undead, so I did not get involved.

Instead, I spent the night meditating on the peak of the roof of my compatriots' new home.

As the sun rose in the eastern sky, casting bright light across the plain and glittering on the glass of the village's many windows, the lingering undead burned up.

I warped down to the street.

Zip.

Looking into the window of the Minecraftians' house, I saw LuckyMist standing inside looking back out at me.

127

The female opened the door and stepped outside to face me in the street. I could see the males standing inside. WolfBroJake was rifling through a chest.

LuckyMist pulled out her compass.

"If you continue south, you'll get there in a little over a day. Well—I don't know—how ever long it takes *you* to get there ... *faster*." She held the compass up closer to me to show me the inner mechanism. "See this *N?*" she asked.

There was a subtle red "N" drawn or carved into the red surface near the edge of the inner disc.

I nodded.

"That's '*north*'. If you hold the compass in front of you and turn around until the needle is on the *N*, then you'll be facing north. You'll need to go *south* to get to the castle, so turn around until the needle is pointing *away* from the *N*. If you keep going in that direction, and be careful to keep the needle pointing directly away from the *N*, you'll keep going south. And when the needle's pointing north, when you're *facing* north, that means that *west* is to your left, and *east* is to your right, but ... I guess you don't need to know *that* to get to the castle." LuckyMist paused, and considered the object in her hand. "I *made* this. Keep it. I'll make another."

She smiled weakly and placed the device into my hand. Her Minecraftian hand was tiny next to my Enderman hand.

I bowed.

"Thank you for the compass, LuckyMist. I will use it, observe the castle, then return."

"Watch your back," WolfBroJake said from inside.

LuckyMist walked back inside, and moved to Xenocide99, who gave her a big hug.

Then, with a **zip**, I teleported out of the village, and started heading south.

As the day brightened and wore on, I warped in small jumps, using the compass at times, travelling always to the south. When I needed to, I stopped to meditate and refresh my *Chi*. I was learning that, over the course of my Seed Stride and this mission to restore the balance, I was getting a lot of practice teleporting, and my connection to my *Chi* was becoming stronger.

It would be a long time before I could just teleport frivolously without worrying about over-exerting myself, but I could warp several times in a row now before I had to slow down to recharge...

By performing a combination of teleporting, walking, and stopping to meditate, I was covering *way* more ground much faster than I did moving with the Minecraftians as a group, and was sure that I would arrive by nightfall.

Then I would approach under cover of darkness...

At one point, later in the day, I happened across a large, black spider in my warping jumps to the south. The creature was exploring idly, and as I reached out with my *Chi* to feel its mind, I found that it was content.

"*Hello, spider*," I said into its mind, approaching on foot from my latest teleport landing.

The creature chittered and hissed, but did not seem aggressive. It stopped, and craned its arachnid neck to look up at my face. I looked down into four bright, glowing red eyes.

"*Hello, Enderman*," it responded in its mind. Its fanged mouth made insectoid sounds. "*Fine day, isn't it?*"

"*Indeed*," I responded. "*Do you live around here?*"

It flexed its fangs. "*I do, yes. I live in a cave nearby.*"

"*What do you know about a skeleton army to the south?*"

The spider shook its furry head with a hiss. "*Don't know anything about an army*," it thought. "*But there is a small group of skeletons that have been passing through here a lot lately. Working together. Strange ones.*"

"Is it strange for them to travel together?" I asked in its mind. *"I've seen skeletons travel in groups of two or three many times. What's strange about them?"*

"Well," thought the spider, *"it's more like a dozen skeletons. They also all wear helmets. Oh, and they all have red eyes!"*

That was indeed strange...

"When was the last time you saw them?" I asked.

"Yesterday, I guess," the spider thought. *"Heading the same way you're headed."*

"Thank you, spider," I said. *"Be well."*

"Wait!" the spider thought, hissing with its mouth. *"What's with the headband? I've never seen an Enderman like you!"*

I instinctively reached to straighten the blue headband and its flowing tails. If I succeeded in my mission, hopefully I wouldn't be wearing it anymore. I was confident that once I defeated the Skeleton King and restored the balance around

Nexus 426 by relocating the Minecraftians back to their castle, that I would be elevated to the rank of *lower ninja*. My initiate blue band, under the white novice-rank symbol, would be replaced with a *black* band. I would finally be a *real* ninja...

"*I am a member of the Order of the Warping Fist, spider. Do you know of it?*"

"*Nope*," the spider answered. "*Well, good day!*" It turned on its eight legs to continue its moseying.

"*One more thing, spider,*" I said in its mind. It turned. "*Stay away from those skeletons. They don't belong here.*"

"*Thanks,*" it thought, then scampered away.

Continuing my journey, warp by warp, jump by jump, I arrived at the Minecraftians' castle before the sun went down.

It was an impressive structure, emerging tall from a valley in the forest ahead of me. Easily large enough to give the three Minecraftians plenty of space, the castle was constructed almost entirely from cobblestone and stone slabs. The top of it was artfully decorated with battlements, and the many windows were adorned with colored glass, save for a large open balcony extending from the top floor of the main section.

The balcony looked down over a courtyard and a large open field full of torches.

Those Minecraftians sure loved their torches...

Around one side of the large structure were fenced-in pens full of animals of all types, as well as a large *farm*—at least I presumed so. The Minecraftians' farm didn't look quite the same as the farm plots in the village. It was much more open and spread out, but had the same rows of dirt broken up by furrows of water. The dirt was bare now, and mostly dry. The entire animal and crop areas were encapsulated by wooden fences.

And the entire castle was *bustling* with skeleton archers.

Skeletons stood guard at the main entrance. Skeletons paced around on the rooftops. A squad of them stood in formation in the courtyard. A few of them were visible on the upper balcony, standing guard at the edges where the extension led into the castle's interior. They walked in the sunlight *without burning*. All of them were armed with bows, and were dressed in chainmail shirts and metal helmets.

Carefully warping around the edge of the property, just inside the darkness of the tree line, I moved around the perimeter of the castle and its outlying areas, finding more groups of skeletons in the back, and arriving back at the front just as a squad of ten skeletons departed to the north together.

Definitely a skeleton army.

It would be a good opportunity to master my *Chi Dodge*. I would have to focus and learn the skill, or be *destroyed* in the forge of battle.

My master's words from one of his lessons drifted into my mind:

"The ninja learns by dwelling on the cutting edge of the sword, standing at the edge of the fire pit, venturing right up to the edge of starvation and

destruction. Vibrant and intense living is the ninja's form of worship..."

Finding a dark place in the forest out of sight from the castle walls, I sat and meditated while waiting for the night to come.

At times, skeleton archer scouts moved through the woods, usually in pairs, but none of them ever came close to me.

As the sun started setting and the valley darkened, I could see glowing, red points of light appearing in the darkness from the army's multiple eyes.

Their eyes really *did* glow red.

Something truly foul was upsetting the balance here. Something, presumably the Skeleton King himself, was a true abomination. A blight on the Overworld. If I did not manage to defeat the Skeleton King and his army, with the help of the Minecraftians, the army would surely spread and throw the Overworld even *more* out of balance as time went on.

For a moment, I contemplated heading back to The End to report to my master and return with reinforcements.

But I let the thought slide over and out of my mind...

No, I thought. He would want me to take care of this on my own. I would be *weak* to go back now, and I'd *never* reach the rank of lower ninja.

Never? a small voice in my mind asked, but I ignored it.

The Skeleton King would be the greatest challenge in this situation. The army was just a bunch of skeletons in armor. No big deal.

No big deal? I thought. *Over a hundred skeleton archers? And you haven't mastered your Chi Dodge yet?*

I shut the doubting voice out of my mind.

I am ninja. I am the warping wind. I could defeat them all—I didn't even *need* the Minecraftians. I would show my master how strong

I really was, and be granted a *higher rank* in the Order...

Just then, the sky changing from pink to blue, I was surprised when a brilliant, red *beam of light* cut into the sky like a laser. A blinding, crimson column of fire! It *speared* into the sky, reaching up, up ... extending forever with the brightness of the sun!

And it came from the castle!

As I stared at the light, the skeleton army cheered and hissed, raising their bows into the air. Looking down at the many archers, I could swear that the red lights in their eyes were suddenly glowing brighter...

What was this technology? What was this magic?

Was it the *source* of the abomination? The source of the corruption? The source of power for the Skeleton King and his army??

I had to take a closer look...

As the sky continued to darken, I waited until the moon was in the sky and the night was at its darkest...

I am ninja. I am a *shadow*.

Zip.

I warped through the forest, staying out of sight of the many glowing red eyes, until I was close enough to warp onto the roof above the balcony.

Zip.

With masterful timing, I teleported into a crook of shadow in the wall above the balcony's roof, but below the battlements. With great stealth, I slithered along the wall, down and around the edge of the roof. Hidden in shadow, I dropped down onto the balcony behind the back of one of the guards.

I slipped through the shadows, sneaking along the wall without a sound, until I had a clear view of the inside of the great, open bedroom just inside the balcony.

The room was bathed in a whispering, crawling red light that came from the base of the gigantic column of brilliance.

It was a large bedroom, or at least, it *used* to be. The room had been modified. *Huge* room. The balcony was designed to allow the Minecraftians inside the room to step outside and look over the courtyard with ease. Now, in the middle of the vast bedroom was a pyramid of metallic blocks—in the red light, it was impossible to tell what kind of metal. But there were *several* blocks, stacked and shining in the red light, and on the peak, at the top of the stack, was some sort of *artifact*—a crystalline object a little smaller than a Minecraftian crafting table. The red light *poured* out of the crystal artifact, straight up into a concentrated column of pure, red light that pierced the sky through an opening in the roof!

As striking as the light artifact was, however, I was most impressed by the Skeleton King himself...

The monster stood in the room directing his skeleton minions as they carried more of the heavy metal blocks over from a corner of the room. In the shadows of the room, spared from the red light, I caught a glint of steel.

Were the blocks made of solid *iron?*

My eyes darted back to the Skeleton King.

The abomination stood twice as tall as the skeletons around him—taller than me. And he was thick and wide, with heavy ribs and dense limbs. The Skeleton King's bones were overall more *massive* than normal skeleton bones, and he had a broad lower jaw that made him appear even more menacing. As I expected, his eyes held the same fierce, red pinpricks of glowing light as the other skeletons. The monster's shoulders were armored, and he held a huge, black bow in one chunky bone hand.

No … not *in* his hand. *On* his hand!

The Skeleton King was armed with a great, black bow that was bolted *sideways* onto a bracer of some kind that was attached to his right arm.

"Move it!" he yelled, his voice like thunder. "Get those blocks in there!"

The skeletal minions struggled with the heavy blocks to finish their work on the pyramid.

Reaching out with my *Chi*, I tried to listen to the energy of the Skeleton King's mind, but it was loud, and *red*, and impossible to read. The artifact must have been blocking me...?

I had seen enough.

There was some sort of powerful, *dark magic* at work here, and the Skeleton King was working hard to increase his power. The column of light was amazing!

I had to get back. Maybe the Minecraftians would know something about this artifact. Maybe if I could neutralize the artifact, it would weaken the Skeleton King, or his entire *army*, or who knows—he might even *die* without it...

Just before I turned to crawl back up the wall, my eye caught something else in the room.

In the back of the bedroom, almost hidden by the glare of the red light, I could barely make out ... iron bars.

Two hands held the bars. All I could see past the bars was a hint of tattered brown robes.

I closed my eyes and, trying to block out the red noise of the artifact, reached out with my *Chi* to feel whatever—or whoever—was trapped in there. I felt a wave of … fear … and …

It was a *villager*. Whoever was behind those bars had the same *villager energy* I felt back in town.

The Skeleton King had a villager *captive* for some reason.

"Yes!!" the Skeleton King cried with his booming voice. "Yes! It's beautiful!!"

Taking care to avoid detection, I slinked away from the interior far enough to allow me to teleport back down to the ground.

Zip.

Warping again with a few small jumps around the perimeter of the castle, I silently ran through the shadows until I was inside the enclosed farm, close to the castle wall. The door that led inside was broken open. From the darkness, I reached out with my *Chi* to feel around the room just inside the castle...

Chests ... Furnaces ...

I opened one of the farm chests that stood in the grass outside, up against the wall. It was full of plant-based things, as well as tools.

Which of these things are food? I thought.

I grabbed droves of items and organic material, and put it all into my dimensional pocket.

Feeling for the presence of enemies inside, I waited until any passing guards were gone, then slinked into the castle from the broken Minecraftian door that led to the farm.

There were several chests, a large pot-thing full of water, and a bank of six furnaces.

Was this the *kitchen* WolfBroJake mentioned?

Opening the nearest chest, I saw that it was full of meat and small dead bodies. I took a large amount of random food-items from the chest and threw it all into my dimensional pocket. Opening another chest across the doorway, I grabbed a lot more of several different items that looked like they might be food, and stored those as well.

The clattering of bones approached, and I slipped out of the doorway back into the night.

The red column of brilliance reaching into the sky from the roof lit up the whole valley with a faint crimson light.

Zip.

I teleported to the tree line. Taking several more jumps from shadow to shadow, I warped through the darkness until I was near the entrance of the courtyard again.

I am the warping wind...

Looking back at the courtyard, I watched as the Skeleton King emerged from the balcony, standing tall like a general above his archer troops down below.

"How's that, my warriors?" he bellowed. "Feel good??"

The undead army cheered.

I turned, took a glance at LuckyMist's compass, then headed north.

Over the rest of the night, I traveled back to the village, warp by warp, jump by jump.

The Skeleton King was impressive, but outside of the awesome appearance of the light artifact, he appeared to be just a giant skeleton. Bigger. Tougher. Harder to kill.

But he *could* be killed.

I would eliminate the Skeleton King, and restore the balance...

Through the course of my jumps back to the village, I passed over the squad of skeletons that I saw depart from the castle earlier. Sticking to the shadows, I warped past them, and they were none the wiser. But I knew where *they* were going...

They were headed to the village.

Day 9 – Overworld

I arrived at the village at dawn, just as the handful of zombies roaming the streets burned up and fell dead, leaving ashes and charred meat on the cobblestone.

Moments after sunlight flooded the plains and started the day, the villagers all sprang from their homes with vigor, bustling about their business with hands together under their robes, muttering to each other in their strange language.

"Hurr … hurr…"

As I stood, observing the dawn from the landing place of my last teleport, a handful of the odd village creatures approached, stopped, looked up at my tall, black form, then turned around and hurried away in the opposite direction.

"He's gotta be there by now!"

It was LuckyMist's voice, hidden within the cluster of buildings.

"I'm sure he's fine," Xenocide99 said. "Don't worry!"

Looking out over the tops of the buildings, it was easy to identify the taller roof of the Minecraftians' new house.

Zip.

I warped onto the peak of their home's roof. Immediately, I sensed the presence of the Minecraftians inside. With an easy step, I dropped off of the roof, landing silently on the cobblestone street down below.

Bending down, I could see the three of them through the window. I reached out into their minds with my *mind voice*.

"I've returned, Minecraftians. Hello, LuckyMist, Xenocide99, and WolfBroJake…"

LuckyMist looked to the window, and smiled when she saw me. The two males looked up from what they were doing, having no idea where I was speaking to them from.

"Elias!" LuckyMist exclaimed. She ran over and opened the door.

Xenocide99 looked over and smiled. He was building something at their crafting table.

"Hey there!" WolfBroJake said. "That was *fast!* Did you go all the way to the castle and back?"

I nodded.

"*I did,*" I said. "*I observed the Skeleton King and his army, their posts and placements around your castle, their patrols,*" I opened my dimensional pocket. "*And I brought you some of your food...*"

"Oh, awesome!!" Xenocide99 exclaimed. He stood. The others similarly perked up. "What'd you bring?"

"Come inside!" LuckyMist said. She stepped aside and motioned for me to follow.

Their wooden entry door was small, but the ceiling inside the house was vaulted and high.

Zip.

I warped in past all of them, leaving a trail of purple motes of light dropping lazily to the floor, surprising them all.

"I picked up many things that I thought may be food for you Minecraftians. From your container in the 'farm' and other containers in what I believe you referred to as your kitchen..."

Xenocide99 pointed to a large, wooden chest in the center of the room. They all backed away from it. "Here, use *this!*" he said.

"Very well," I replied, and opened the chest. It was empty. Looking into my dimensional pocket, I dumped the huge amount of dead bodies and miscellaneous organic materials and resources I gathered from the castle into the container.

I stepped back, and they all approached the chest to see what was inside.

"Let's see," LuckyMist said. "Some ... cooked chicken—good! *Lots* of pork chops, raw rabbit meat and ... *spider eyes?*" She laughed.

"What the—?" Xenocide99 said. "Ink sacs from the squids? Golden apples? That's not *food!*"

"Hey, here's some carrots," WolfBroJake said. He looked at Xenocide99. "Knock it off! He probably doesn't know what we *eat*, right? Here's some bones ... there's like a *hundred* bones!" He chuckled to himself.

LuckyMist was pulling out some of the dead meat and plant materials, and setting it aside.

"So let's see," she said. "All in all, food-wise, we've got a few dozen pieces of cooked chicken, around *sixty* pork chops, rabbit meat to cook, *lots* of wheat, dozens of carrots, a handful of cooked pieces of salmon ... this is *great!*" She turned to me. "You did great, Elias! Thank you!"

WolfBroJake turned to me. "Yeah, Ninja, you got a bunch of stuff that's not food, but you got tons of food, too. We're *set*. Thanks!"

Xenocide99 smiled and made some sort of Minecraftian gesture at me while eating a piece of chicken.

After a while, the three of them had organized all of the items I brought back from the castle into the various chests in the house, and put several pieces of food in their packs, as I sat on the floor in an empty space to meditate.

"So what did you see?" WolfBroJake asked me.

They all turned, and I related the tale of what I saw in the castle. I told them about the skeleton archers positioned in several places around the grounds, patrols, sentries, about the balcony and the Skeleton King inside having his troops build the pyramid of iron in their large room. I told them about the artifact and the blazing beam of red light. The glowing eyes. The captive villager...

"Wow," Xenocide99 said, staring at the floor. "Sounds like he's really built himself up a *lot*. *Way* more skeletons than the force that chased us off before..."

"What's with the metal blocks around the artifact?" LuckyMist asked her friends.

"Something about that sounds familiar," WolfBroJake said, thinking to himself.

152

"Yeah, last time we saw the artifact it wasn't on top of metal blocks..."

"*You were aware of the artifact?*" I asked into their minds.

"Yeah," Xenocide99 said. "We saw the light before we met the Skeleton King."

WolfBroJake turned to me and spoke up. He was still avoiding eye contact. Both of the males were still avoiding looking me in the eye. "When the skeletons attacked at first, they *killed* us. We were surprised. When we *respawned* in the bedroom up top, they were already taking over the inside of the castle, and attacked us up there before we could get any armor on—"

"Yeah," LuckyMist said, shaking her head. "That was *crazy*..."

"So we fell back to a little cave nearby to regroup," WolfBroJake said. "That's when we saw the red light, shooting up into the sky!"

"And that's when *he* showed up," Xenocide99 said.

"Yeah," LuckyMist said. "When the red light came on, the Skeleton King was suddenly in our room, and came out on the balcony to, like ... *rally* the skeletons. Their eyes all turned red, and—"

"It was like nothing we'd ever seen!" WolfBroJake said. "We," he referred to himself and Xenocide99, "ran back to the courtyard, where we died the first time, to get our gear and armor. We got *some* of it, enough to try to make another attack to get inside."

"And the Skeleton King *kicked our butts*," Xenocide99 said. "And he *laughed* at us!"

"That's when we left and tried to start over in the cave," LuckyMist said.

"*What do you believe is the connection between the artifact and the Skeleton King?*" I asked. "*From what I observed and from what you've described, it sounds like they are connected...*"

WolfBroJake looked up, then quickly averted his eyes.

LuckyMist gasped, thinking to herself.

154

"Of course!" WolfBroJake said. "That evil red light artifact must be some sort of *portal* or something!"

"Or the source of his power," LuckyMist said.

"If the skeletons have been building it up with metal blocks..." Xenocide99 said.

"*I agree*," I said. "*It's possible that the Skeleton King derives his power from the artifact. And if he has been building it up with those blocks, to enhance the power somehow, he might—*"

I stopped.

The Minecraftians hung on my words, waiting for me to complete my sentence.

They did not detect it. But I did.

We were being watched.

Reaching out with my *Chi*, I listened to the energy of the village around me. Fear. Urgency. There was a villager standing *just outside* the front door, eavesdropping...

Standing without a sound, I warped out of the open door, and immediately towered over ... the village blacksmith!

He startled, looking up at me with widened eyes. His flat lips parted, and his mouth hung open for a moment in surprise. The villager leaned back, and made a small sound of shock.

"Hurr!"

"What's going on?" Xenocide99 asked from inside.

Reaching into the villager's weird mind, cutting through the strange mental walls of alien energy surrounding his thoughts, I spoke to him.

"What is it, villager? Why do you spy on us?"

The villager stumbled backwards, and gripped the cobblestone wall behind him.

"Dark One, you speak in my head? Do not hurt me, please!!"

As I pulled the meaning of his words from his mind, his mouth made the sounds of the

156

villager language. The Minecraftians only heard, "Hurr, hmm hurr? Huh Hmm!"

"He's talking to a villager!" said LuckyMist from inside.

The three of them ran up to watch from the doorway and windows.

"*Be calm, villager,*" I said. As I spoke, I reached out to the minds of the Minecraftians so that *they too* would understand the conversation. "*Who are you? What are you doing listening to us?*"

The villager gulped, pressing his wide lips together. His brow raised in alarm, but I could sense that he was trying to relax.

"*My name is Kumara, Dark One! I am the apprentice blacksmith! I was wondering… what you heroes were doing … in our village?*"

"Wow, this is wild," Xenocide99 said. I can understand him, even though he's just talking like a normal villager!"

"You too?" LuckyMist asked.

"I've never talked to a villager for *real* before!" Xenocide99 said.

"You still haven't, doofus!" WolfBroJake said. "We're just listening. Be *quiet!*"

"*Heros?*" I responded.

Kumara blanched, suddenly afraid. "*You're … not heroes? Are you with … the undead army?*"

What did the *villagers* know about the undead army?

The four of us had approached this situation as if we were the only ones affected by the abomination to the south. All this time, the *village* may have been involved, too. If this villager wasn't listening in, and I didn't ask him about it, we might have lost out on some valuable intelligence…

I suddenly remembered Xenocide99 pointing out that the farms were all empty. That it was out of the ordinary.

"*We are not with the undead army, Kumara,*" I said. "*In fact, we are opposed to their presence in this region. What do you know of them? What do you know of the Skeleton King?"*

The blacksmith gulped. His eyes darted around, then he looked back up at me.

"I don't know of a Skeleton King, Dark One. But the red-eyed skeletons have been visiting us regularly for a few days now."

"And what do they do here?"

"They take our iron. All of it. We have been suffering from the shortage, Dark One..."

"What are they getting *iron* for?" Xenocide99 asked.

"For their *armor*, probably," WolfBroJake said.

I looked at the Minecraftians, then back down to the villager.

"Do you know why they take your iron?"

"At first," Kumara said, *"they were having me and my master, Balder, craft armor shirts. Helmets. And solid blocks of iron. Now that my*

159

master is with them, they just come for the iron ingots."

"OMG, *with them?*" LuckyMist asked with a gasp. "That was the *prisoner* you saw?" she asked me.

"Helmets for moving around during the day…" WolfBroJake said.

"*Why is your master with them?*" I asked.

"*They took him to punish us,*" Kumara said. He perked up. "*My master is alive??*"

"*He is,*" I responded. "*I saw him there. He must be building the blocks and armor for them at the castle now.*"

"*That is good news!*" Kumara said. "*Oh, I hope you can rescue him and bring him back to the village??*"

"Of course we will!" LuckyMist exclaimed.

"We'll *try,*" WolfBroJake said.

Kumara spoke up again. "*At first, when they came, my master refused to hand over our iron. So they destroyed our crops, and we did what they wanted. We worked all day building helmets and iron blocks for the army to take away with them. The next time they came, we tried to hide some of our iron.*" Kumara looked down at his feet. "*Well, I tried to hide it, at least. When the army found it, they took all of the iron and took my master away with them. Please, you* must *save him! It is my fault that he was kidnapped!*"

No one spoke for a moment.

"*They are coming again,*" I said into their minds. "*Today. I encountered the patrol on the way back here during the night...*"

The villager paled. "*Yesterday I created twenty-one iron ingots from all of the iron ore we had remaining. But now ... you all are here! You can kill the skeletons and rescue my master!*"

"How many did you see again in the patrol?" WolfBroJake asked me.

"*Ten,*" I responded.

"We can *totally* take out ten skeletons!" Xenocide99 said. "Even if they're wearing helmets and chain shirts!"

"Guys..." LuckyMist said.

I thought for a moment. While I and the Minecraftians could certainly defeat a group of ten skeletons without casualty, if the squad did not report back to the Skeleton King when they were expected, there would be more—maybe the entire force, led by the abomination himself. They would make an *example* out of this village, and slaughter them all...

While it was true that if the Skeleton King divided his forces, say, to send half of his army here and keep the other half at the castle, it would be easier to defeat *each group*, it was still quite a risk to the villagers.

I felt that, if the artifact was a *portal link*, or some sort of magical device giving the Skeleton King his power, then the best course of action would be to steal or destroy it before engaging him. Heck—removing or breaking the artifact may actually destroy or banish the Skeleton King

162

himself, and then it would be fairly easy to defeat and disband his army!

"*We must not ruin the element of surprise*," I said to them all. "*When the skeleton squad arrives, we must hide and wait. We'll let them take the iron, and let them go back to the castle. We must only intervene if they start killing villagers…*"

Kumara gulped and looked quite disappointed after that, deflated and staring back at the ground.

"Are you *nuts?!*" WolfBroJake said. "We can take them out, then head to the castle and fight the army with ten less skeletons!"

Xenocide99 and LuckyMist were shocked that WolfBroJake was so brash with me.

"*And if our assault fails*," I replied, "*then the Skeleton King will know that the village was involved*."

"He's right," LuckyMist said. "Then there'd be no village *left*…"

"Well," WolfBroJake said, looking at Kumara, "Can we at least have *some* iron before he gives it all away to the bad guys?? It would be good to build some shields for everyone—you know, since we'll be fighting an army of *archers* after all..."

I looked at Kumara.

"*Will you supply the Minecraftians with some iron for their armor? We will do everything we can to destroy the army and return your master to the village...*"

"*Yeah, sure,*" Kumara said. "*I guess the skeletons won't know any better...*"

Before the skeleton squad came any closer, WolfBroJake accompanied Kumara to the village forge, and came back a short time later with three brand-new shields for the group.

"Are you sure you don't want one too, Ninja?" he asked.

I shook my head.

"*My spirit is the true shield,*" I said.

164

Over the course of the day, we made plans for the attack. The Minecraftians knew of a cave, their *old* home back before they built the castle, a place that was near enough to stage the attack from. It would take the entire day, tomorrow, for us all to travel to the cave together. The skeleton squad would be arriving back at the castle just ahead of us, presuming all went smoothly and they headed straight back there after stealing the village's iron.

In the morning, when the Skeleton King would likely be preoccupied with having the captive blacksmith create new things with the iron, we would *attack!*

As the Minecraftians launch a frontal attack on the skeleton army, I would warp into the bedroom with the artifact, and do what I could to disable or destroy it. If the Skeleton King remained, I would defeat him myself in *martial combat*, then rejoin the others to complete the battle.

I would find victory, and succeed in my mission.

I would be promoted to *lower ninja*...

The skeleton squad arrived in the afternoon.

I could sense that the Minecraftians were very troubled to hide and not intervene. They crouched under the windows of their home, holding their swords in twitchy hands, and my *Chi* picked up on their angry energy.

The villagers, on the other hand, were very afraid. As soon as the squad arrived, marching in a tight, militant group, the inhabitants of the town fled in every direction, staying as far away from the undead as they could.

The skeletons transitioned into a single-file line, the sun gleaming on their helmets and chainmail shirts, and, holding their bows at the ready, they marched down the cobblestone streets to the blacksmith building without a word.

I watched it all from the shadows of a nearby tree.

The archers' energy was simple. Determined, dangerous, and *red*. Always the *red energy* with this abomination army. There was no fear, no insecurity, no uncertainty—they were like *machines*.

When the undead arrived at the blacksmith's, I reached out with my *mind voice*, and spoke to Kumara.

"*Remember,*" I said, "*Stay calm, and don't let them know that you know about your captive master...*"

From my vantage point, I could see Kumara meekly step aside as the lead skeleton pushed past him through the doorway. The skeleton archer must have been satisfied, because when it emerged into the street again, the column of skeletons turned around, and marched out to the edge of town.

For a moment, I thought that they might have detected something *off*, because they stopped before leaving the areas around the farm plots, looked back and peered around the town, before finally turning and marching back into the forest.

But they left, and didn't stop until they disappeared into the forest.

Zip.

I warped back into town.

After the villagers recovered and continued their business, I could sense a sad energy about them. Kumara himself, on the other hand, was relived and hopeful.

Over the course of the evening, the Minecraftians prepared all of the gear and food they would take with them, working in silence, thinking about what was to come...

Day 10 – Overworld

We departed on our day's journey as soon as the sun was up.

The Minecraftians' energy was grim.

I could sense that they put a lot of their hope in *me*, and were afraid of losing what little they had left if we failed.

If we failed.

I felt confident in my abilities. The Skeleton King was just an oversized skeleton archer—he was no match for an Enderman Ninja of the *Order of the Warping Fist*…

Following the compass LuckyMist gave me, we walked all day, and I stayed with them on foot. Even though I could cross the distance to the castle quickly and easily, these poor Minecraftians' technology was a long way off from harnessing the power of the pearl.

"Remember," WolfBroJake was telling LuckyMist, "the shield will slow you down. You'll have to be careful to only raise it when you think the skeleton is about to shoot you."

"*Your shield*," I said to them, "*is similar to my Chi Dodge*."

"What is a *Chi Dodge?*" Xenocide99 asked.

I contemplated that concept for a moment. It was similar, and it also *wasn't*. The Minecraftians had to raise their shields, on purpose, for each attack they intended to deflect. Every time I dodged an arrow, it was similar. I would see the arrow coming, and warp out of the way. And I was getting better at the *Dodge* for every battle I got into here on the Overworld.

But it *wasn't* like the shield in the way that the *Chi Dodge*, when mastered, was performed by instinct.

I should not be raising my shield on purpose.

My shield should defend me *without* effort...

I repeated my master's words to myself, and to the Minecraftians in their minds:

"Do not learn to try harder. The key is to learn how not to try in the first place..."

"What?!" Xenocide99 said. "That doesn't make sense..."

"The Enderman doesn't even have to *worry* about arrows," WolfBroJake said. "You just teleport out of the way of them, don't you?" He looked up at me for a moment, then, as if forgetting something, immediately averted his eyes.

"Not always," LuckyMist said quietly. "He was hit by one of Xenocide99's arrows."

"Oh yeah..." Xenocide99 said. "Why is that?" He looked up at me, then turned away.

"I don't know why you guys are still *doing* that," LuckyMist said.

"Doing what?" WolfBroJake asked.

"Looking away!" she exclaimed. "Avoiding eye contact with Elias. He's *clearly* not a normal

171

Enderman—*duh!*" She looked up at me. "I've never seen their purple eyes so close before actually..."

"*It's true,*" I said to them. "*You don't have to avert your eyes.*"

WolfBroJake looked up at me. I could sense his nervousness, but he eventually connected his eyes with mine. Xenocide99 followed suit, and I turned to look down at him too.

"Why?" WolfBroJake asked. "Everyone *knows* not to look an Enderman in the eye. They attack."

"*My Ender race is an old, powerful race, one with very strong passions,*" I said. "*While what you say may be true, that it is unwise for one of the lower races to look the typical Enderman in the eye—*"

"*Lower* races??" Xenocide99 asked. LuckyMist shushed him.

"*I am a member of the Order of the Warping Fist. We are the protectors of the race, and we enhance our power by mastering the skills of the ninja and martial arts. To protect the Ender*

172

race, we are also charged with maintaining the neutrality of the Overworld. That is why I am here, why I defeated you before, and why I am setting out to defeat the Skeleton King now. We must destroy the abominations that upset the balance of the Overworld."

"But why don't you get angry like the others?" LuckyMist asked.

"*The inner power of an Ender is strong. In normal Endermen, it boils up easily, and makes them fearsome opponents. But we, of the Order, have learned to harness the power of that rage and channel it into our martial skills while increasing the strength and reach of our Chi. I maintain a clear mind through meditation and contemplation, so no … looking into my eyes will not make me angry.*"

"How do ninjas of … *the Order* … control *their* anger?" WolfBroJake asked.

"He just *said*, doofus!" Xenocide99 said. "Through meditation and contemplation!"

WolfBroJake punched Xenocide99 in the shoulder.

"Oww!" he cried.

"*Shut up*, you guys!" LuckyMist said.

"*We control the rage power by attaining wisdom,*" I said.

"How do you attain wisdom?" WolfBroJake said.

"*With a still mind,*" I said. "*We acquire a still mind by keeping calm and controlling emotion. We acquire focus by applying a still mind to separate the important from the unimportant, and while pursuing tasks. We acquire knowledge by applying focus to tasks to the best of ability. And we acquire wisdom by applying knowledge with focus, along with a still mind...*"

They walked with me in silence for a moment.

"Mind ... blown ..." Xenocide99 said suddenly.

"Yeah, that sounds complicated," WolfBroJake said. "Sounds hard to perfect for sure..."

174

"*The true work of martial arts,*" I said, "*is progress, not perfection.*"

"You still didn't explain that *Chi Dodge*," LuckyMist said.

"*For me,*" I responded, "*that is still a work in progress...*"

We walked and chatted about other things for the rest of the day.

When we passed where I met the friendly spider, we did not see the creature. It had either moved on, or was inside its cave, or it was *hiding* from the Minecraftians, who would have surely tried to kill it.

In time, we reached our destination.

"We're here!" LuckyMist exclaimed. "I recognize this place!"

"Oh yeah..." said Xenocide99. "There's the *boot rock*. The entrance should be right over..."

The Minecraftians left our southerly course and meandered through the woods for a moment.

Xenocide99 had pointed to a natural formation of stone in between some trees that was shaped like an *L*. I could see how they interpreted the shape as one of their Minecraftian *boots*.

"Here it is!" said WolfBroJake.

Zip.

I warped over to where they stood, and saw a small, dirt opening, leading into the ground. It could have been like any other cave, except it was made from stacked dirt blocks, and the hole into the darkness below was just the right size for a wooden door.

The three of them happily ran into the dirt opening, down the crude dirt stairs, and into the dark. Immediately, I heard the Minecraftians placing torches on the walls, and a soft glow emanated from within.

I wouldn't be able to fit through the opening without crawling through the hole. It was likely that the ceiling was too low to hold me anyway.

We talked a little more until nightfall about the plan of attack. LuckyMist offered to hollow out more of their cave's ceiling so that I could fit, but I was content to stay outside for the night, meditating.

When the sun went down, instead of placing a door and possibly drawing attention from skeleton scouts, the Minecraftians instead blocked up their entrance with dirt, and were gone— entombed in the ground for the night.

I teleported to the top of a tree and watched the stars for a while.

In the distance, I could see the bright column of red light stabbing into the sky. I had a *bad feeling* about that artifact—but the feeling was not rational, so I let it slip away...

After watching the red light for a while, I settled into my meditation posture, and closed my eyes.

The coming day would require my *Chi* to be fully recharged.

And to fight the archers, I would need my full concentration—I would need to try hard to master the *Chi Dodge*.

Letting my *Chi* grow and flow over me like water, I waited for the morning.

Day 11 – Overworld

In the morning, we were ready.

The Minecraftians woke up just before the dawn, breaking open their little dirt blockade while the world was still dark blue.

Of course, I thought. They didn't have any way to know when morning came. They wouldn't be able to see the light from inside the cave.

Once the sun finished rising, they stepped out of their little dirt home.

I briefly wondered, looking down at the crude dwelling, that if this was their first home before they built the castle, where did they come from *before* they lived here?

"Elias?" LuckyMist called, looking around in the forest. They didn't bother looking up into the trees.

Taking care to conserve my *Chi* energy for the battle, I leapt down from the treetop, landing silently in the grass.

"*I am here,*" I said into their minds. "*Are you all ready?*"

"Everybody good on food?" asked WolfBroJake.

"Yes," said LuckyMist. Xenocide99 nodded.

"Let's go," WolfBroJake said.

We all walked together to the castle, taking care to be quiet. I walked without a sound, of course. The Minecraftians were far from silent, but they were careful, and weren't making too much noise. Not bad for being decked out in armor and shields...

I could tell that the three of them were quite familiar with their surroundings. I never had to check my compass—I just followed them, staying concealed in the early morning shadows of the trees. Even if they didn't know where they were going, I still had a pretty good idea of where the castle was because of the red column of light cutting through the night sky that I watched during my meditation.

Whenever there was a break in the trees, I could still *see* the red light, too, bright even against the clear, blue sky.

Eventually, keeping away from the skeleton scouts with my guidance, we found ourselves at the edge of the castle grounds, just inside the shadows of the tree line, looking over the army of undead and the castle courtyard.

There must have been at least thirty skeletons standing idle in the courtyard, and at least a dozen others stationed at various points at the castle's entrances and up on the battlements. There were probably more around the back, as well as inside. I didn't investigate the entire castle interior, either, nor did I think to ask the Minecraftians about it. All I saw inside the cobblestone walls, the last time I was here, was the large bedroom, and the kitchen.

"Are you ready?" I asked them. *"I will join you in the initial battle to create the diversion and draw the army, then I will warp to the artifact room. You will have to fight them for a while, until I destroy or steal the device..."*

"Are we ready to fight a hundred-whatever skeletons??" Xenocide99 asked. "Oh yeah, sure, we do this sort of thing *all the time!*"

The Minecraftian's tone was odd, and I didn't understand what he meant. Surely he wasn't serious...

WolfBroJake smirked. "Yeah, we're ready. Let's rock."

All three of them were looking up at the column of brilliant, red light, piercing the sky as high as we could see.

"*LuckyMist?*" I asked, looking down at her. She held her shield and sword. I sensed that she was terrified. "*Ready?*"

"Yeah," she said. "As ready as I'll ever be. Be careful when you get in there."

WolfBroJake started breathing hard, huffing, flexing his arms. Xenocide99 stood from his crouch, probably sensing that his buddy was about to spring into action.

"Let's go!!" WolfBroJake cried, bursting out of the trees. "Raaaarrrr!!" he cried, holding his sword high and his shield in front of him as he *charged* into the large group of skeleton archers.

Xenocide99 broke into a run next to him, raising his iron blade and letting loose a similar battle cry, sprinting straight at the army! LuckyMist ran along with him, quiet and focused, holding her shield, readying her sword.

As the Minecraftians clashed into the skeleton force, swords cutting into bone and sending pieces of the undead flying, I warped into the middle of the archers to take out as many as I could before risking being seen by the Skeleton King.

The abomination would not really be surprised by a Minecraftian attack, but if he saw an *Enderman* battling his troops alongside *with them*, in broad daylight, he would be wary.

I stood surrounded by the group of skeletons for a split second, while several glowing red eyes fixed on me in confusion, before my fists and feet began to fly.

183

A powerful palm strike immediately knocked one of the skeletons backwards into others, and three of them clattered to the ground. My other hand rapidly knocked the bow out of the bony fingers of another skeleton, then lashed in a fist, connecting with the undead creature's head. The archer's helmet flew off and skittered away on the ground, and the skeleton burst into flames. I sent a powerful roundhouse kick into a *third* adversary, and, even though the archer was armored with a chainmail shirt, I felt its chest crush under my foot, and it fell to the ground in a shower of bones!

Several bows raised to fire at me.

Zip.

Suddenly in another area, surrounded by more skeletons, I heard my previous opponents fire arrows at nothing but thin air.

My new opponents reacted in shock, and I sent a combination of palm strikes with blinding speed into another skeleton, crunching its body under my blows and sending it flying backwards into its comrades. I leapt at a new adversary,

184

landing my knee in its chest and driving it to the ground. Its thin, skeletal legs buckled, and I crushed the archer into a pile of bones before leaping back to my feet.

The skeleton army was like an angry bee's nest now, swarming, and reacting as best as it could to the *surprise attack*. The small army was splitting off into even smaller groups now, aiming bows deliberately, and firing arrows here and there.

With the entire group of undead on the move, I heard their bones clattering around me like the fall of rain in a storm...

Off to my left, I could hear the *thunks* of arrows hitting the shields of the Minecraftians. I also heard the crunch of their swords sinking into their foes. They were yelling at each other.

"Behind you!" The voice of WolfBroJake.

"Got it, thanks!" The voice of Xenocide99.

I could sense their energy, being swarmed by the *red Chi* of the abomination army, and for

185

now, the Minecraftians felt fine to me. They were doing well.

A bow fired from somewhere close to me.

Zip.

I appeared in another place, close to a cluster of skeletons moving off together.

Pay attention! I thought. I would have to try hard and *focus*, or I'd be full of arrows in no time!

With another powerful palm strike, I smashed another skeleton into pieces. Then I kicked another, one that stood at the edge of the group, sending the archer flying and *crashing* into the cobblestone wall of the castle, where it shattered into bones...

I could *do* this. No problem. We would win.

"What's going on out here?" a booming voice called from above me.

That's my cue, I thought.

Zip.

I teleported back into the shadows of the trees, a good distance away from the battle.

Glancing back, I looked over the fight...

The Minecraftians were standing strong tight together, holding up shields covered in arrows, protecting each other's flanks, and surrounded by a surprising amount of shattered bones and dropped bows and arrows.

The skeleton army was converging upon them, but they were *fine*. Xenocide99 and LuckyMist had an arrow or two stuck in their armor, but all three of them were unharmed and fighting well.

I could see a few isolated areas where I had been fighting, the evidence of my *own* little teleporting battles shown by small piles of bones here and there in the courtyard.

The Skeleton King stood on the balcony, his thick, bony hands grasping the railing, leaning over and watching the battle. He looked angry, then smiled, his red eyes burning. From behind him, the red light of the artifact blazed in the otherwise dark room.

"Destroy them!" the Skeleton King bellowed, then turned back. "Prisoner! Install the last block! Start the *new power!*" He turned back to the battle outside, and leaned over, watching eagerly.

Just then, my *Chi* surged, and I could feel the *red energy* increase dramatically. The noise surrounding my pearl made me dizzy for a moment. I felt a strange sense of time changing, and was shocked to see the skeleton army, all of the individual undead archers, bedecked in their armor and wielding their wooden bows … *speed up*.

I could hear the Minecraftians crying out in surprise.

"What's happening?" Xenocide99 cried over the noise.

"They're going faster!" WolfBroJake yelled. "Stay focused! Don't let the arrows get through!"

They yelled commands at each other, and tried to stay on top of the battle as the skeletons all started running instead of walking. Firing faster. Recovering faster.

The Skeleton King watched from the balcony and smiled broadly with his thick jaw.

"Yes!" the abomination exclaimed. "Yes! Ha HA!! Kill them! Kill them all!!"

Something bad was happening.

The artifact was the center of it. I had to do something or the Minecraftians would be overwhelmed and die...

Zip.

Just like I did the other night, I teleported straight to the area of the castle wall in between the balcony roof and the battlements above.

The Skeleton King didn't seem to notice, and he stood at the edge of the balcony with his massive back turned to me.

Clinging to the wall with ease, I slipped down onto the balcony behind a skeleton guard, just like I did before.

Looking into the room, I saw the column of red light, brilliant and burning, shooting up through the roof and into the sky, bathing the entire large room with a red glare.

Unlike the other night, I saw a couple of skeleton archers leading the captive villager blacksmith back to his cage. The prisoner looked very similar to Kumara, dressed the same in brown and black, but was bruised and dirty.

The pyramid of iron blocks seemed to be one level higher than it was the last time I saw it.

Or was it just my imagination?

I could hear the battle down below over the booming laughter of the Skeleton King. I could hear the Minecraftians' shields taking arrows, and the sounds of their swords breaking bones.

They were shouting at each other, half-panicked.

I had to do something.

Kill the Skeleton King. Destroy the artifact. *Help* them.

With the balcony guards facing outside, and the skeletons inside tending to the blacksmith, the captive Balder, *no one* was watching the artifact. *No one* was watching the Skeleton King...

Zip.

I warped to the middle of the room, halfway between the Skeleton King on the balcony, and the artifact with its red column of light.

The Skeleton King was big and heavy. It would take all of my strength to knock him down from the balcony. I didn't believe that the fall would kill him, not with the artifact still active, but I *knew* that I could best him.

After all, the bigger they are, the harder they fall...

Taking a running start, I flew across the distance on silent feet like a shadow of death, leaped into the air without a sound, and with a

191

mighty *kiai* battle cry, I landed a *flying dragon kick* square in the middle of the Skeleton King's back!

With a bellow, the monster cried out in pain and alarm.

It was like kicking a stone wall.

I felt the thick, heavy bones crunch under my foot, and the Skeleton King's arms flailed out to catch his balance.

My flying kick struck *true*, though, and the huge skeleton tumbled over the railing, crying out with his booming voice!

As the Skeleton King disappeared over the ledge, the other four skeletons in the room turned toward me in surprise.

I am the warping wind...

Zip.

Suddenly, I was standing behind the artifact. The brilliance of the red beam of light was blinding my eyes! The red noise of its energy was clouding my *Chi*.

With another *kiai* cry, I focused all of my energy into a powerful palm strike, and struck the artifact straight on.

Something *snapped* under it, and the brilliant light in my face was suddenly *gone!*

The device tumbled down the iron block pyramid and slid across the cobblestone floor.

I did it!

I disabled the artifact!

The Skeleton King was down below, hopefully dead, and the artifact was disabled. Its power was *off*. The skeleton army should lose their *speed* power, and maybe even turn into normal skeletons again!

Suddenly, I felt the stab of an arrow sink into my right leg. The pain shocked me, and I cursed inside.

I forgot about the skeleton guards!

Running down the pyramid like a fleeting shadow, I bolted across the cobblestone floor, and scooped up the dead artifact. It was heavy and smooth, and cold as ice.

I heard the twang of another bow in the room.

Zip.

Now in the opposite corner of the room, I took a quick second to throw the artifact into my dimensional pocket as the skeleton guards adjusted their aim. Once the artifact was secure, I sprinted to the nearest archer.

I am the warping w—!

I stumbled. The arrow in my leg stopped my attack. I couldn't run! Not in battle, anyway.

No matter.

Zip.

I teleported to behind the nearest skeleton, and pummeled him with palm strikes until he fell, scattered bones. Other arrows flew through the air at me.

Zip.

Suddenly, I was behind another archer, and with a mighty strike of my fist, I knocked its skull off of its bony body. It fell.

Zip.

Now close to another, I punched at it once, crunching bones in its chest, then used my other hand to knock its bow out of its grip and onto the floor.

Then I watched with amazement as the bones of its chest mended and *regenerated* before my eyes!

What?!

I pummeled it with multiple rapid strikes, and sent its bones scattering across the floor. It fell.

Looking for the last remaining skeleton, I saw it in the corner of the room just before it fired.

Zip.

The bow twanged, and the skeleton shot at open air. Behind the archer suddenly, I pounded it into bone dust!

My enemies in this room were vanquished. Before joining the Minecraftians to finish the battle though, there was *one more thing* up here that I needed to do.

With the room quiet now, I could hear him.

"Hurr! Hmm … hurr!!"

The master blacksmith, Balder, cried out for help from behind the iron bars of his cage. Walking quickly to the impromptu prison, I was reminded again by the pain in my leg that I would have to avoid sprinting in the fight outside.

Looking over the bars and the door of the cage, I toyed with the metal lock.

I could break this...

Winding up for a mighty *block-breaking strike*, I let loose a loud *kiai* and smashed the lock with my fist. The cage door fell open.

"Get out of here!" I said into Balder's mind. *"Get outside and hide until the skeletons are destroyed!"*

The beaten and dirty blacksmith put his hands together under his robes and furrowed his brow.

"Hmmph!" he said, and ran through the archway in the corner of the room and down the stairs.

Walking to the balcony to where I could once again see the battle, I pulled the arrow from my leg, and joined the Minecraftians.

Zip.

They were holding up better than I thought. No one was injured.

"Elias! Ohmygod!" LuckyMist exclaimed, looking up at me from under her helmet. She had several arrows stuck in her armor, and her shield was like a *porcupine*.

By now, all of the skeletons from the entire property, except maybe the ones on the roof, had come to the courtyard and joined in the battle. There were … maybe … a hundred? A large force, to be sure.

All around the three mighty Minecraftians were piles upon piles of bones, bows, and arrows. They had killed countless archers while I was inside.

But there was one problem.

The skeletons were still moving unnaturally fast...

Thunk!

"Rrraaarrr!" I roared with my natural Enderman voice as an arrow pierced my body.

The battle was far from over, and I didn't know the *Chi Dodge!*

I would have to focus intensely and warp out of the way of every single arrow coming at me!

While I contemplated the *Chi Dodge*, I pummeled the nearest skeleton into clattering bones.

I moved like the wind, even though my injured leg slowed me down. My fists and feet were a flurry of darkness, lashing out at the enemies all around me, breaking bones and

198

shattering my opponents. When I didn't destroy an opponent immediately with my strikes, I could see that their bones were mending and my damage was being undone.

"*They are still regenerating!*" I cried out into the Minecraftians' minds.

"Yeah, they're healing!" WolfBroJake yelled. "I don't get it! You took down the artifact, didn't you?"

Zip.

I teleported to dodge an arrow.

Zip.

Warped to dodge another.

My fists lashed out and destroyed another skeleton.

"*I did!*" I said. "*I took the artifact with me. The Skeleton King—*"

I quickly peered over the battle to the balcony, then to the ground below it…

The abomination's body lay in the dirt, a huge pile of thick, massive bones, squirming in death.

An arrow was coming at me.

Zip.

That was close, I thought.

Wait—squirming?!

I took a moment to use a combination of palm strikes and kicks from my good leg to take out a couple of skeletons, then looked again.

And I saw the Skeleton King climbing to his feet...

The monster stood, moved his arms to loosen up his shoulders, and cracked his neck side to side. His eyes settled onto the battle, and the red lights inside blazed brightly when they turned to *me*.

"You *fools!!*" the Skeleton King bellowed from across the courtyard.

"He's still alive!" LuckyMist shrieked.

And then her shield broke to pieces!

One too many arrows...

She let out a cry of pain as an arrow hit a weak spot in her armor.

"LuckyMist!" Xenocide99 cried, and he moved to protect her, holding his shield against the constant barrage of arrows.

"My *beacon!*" the Skeleton King roared. "What did you do to it?!"

Zip.

I warped out of the way of another arrow coming at me, then destroyed a couple more skeletons with rapid strikes.

Venturing a look back to the Minecraftians, I saw Xenocide99 doing what he could to protect LuckyMist, who was trying to take out the skeletons closest to her with a sword and *no shield*.

WolfBroJake was somehow separated from the other two—probably when LuckyMist's shield was broken—and he was now doing the best he could to kill the archers around him without becoming surrounded.

This was turning bad in a hurry!

Looking back to the Skeleton King, my attention was taken suddenly by another skeleton aiming at me. I wouldn't have time to stop him before he fired.

Zip.

I teleported out of the way, and crushed the nearest new skeleton with a fierce kick.

None of it mattered. I was a member of the Order of the Warping Fist. I could save them. I could defeat the Skeleton King and this entire army on my *own* if I had to!

Just then, I looked back at the Skeleton King just in time to see the abomination aiming his monstrous, sideways *black bow* at the Minecraftians. An arrow appeared out of thin air and was drawn back as if by magic, then launched through the air with great speed at...

It was more like a spear than an arrow, and when it hit the unsuspecting Xenocide99, it cut *right through* his armor. He cried out in pain and surprise, and was killed instantly, disappearing in a flash of smoke!

"Nooo!" WolfBroJake cried. LuckyMist screamed, and stood, shocked, full exposed.

The Skeleton King laughed, his deep voice booming across the battle.

Zip.

I teleported to LuckyMist, and launched a flurry of attacks at the nearest skeletons.

They were still *fast!*

But I was faster!

"Grab his shield!" I yelled into her mind.

An arrow flew at me, but I knew in that instant that if I warped out of the way, it would hit LuckyMist.

Spinning like a whirlwind, I batted the arrow out of midair with my hand!

That was *too* close…

LuckyMist finally stirred into action, swooping down into Xenocide99's gear to pick up his shield, but cried in pain as she was shot in the back.

WolfBroJake grunted in pain as an arrow made it through his defenses, wounding his sword arm.

"I'm coming!" the warrior cried, as he pushed his way through the mass of skeletons, cutting through them as best he could. He cried out in pain as he was struck again.

We were surrounded.

Twang!

Zip.

I warped out of the way and destroyed another two skeletons with a series of palm strikes.

"They're too fast!!" LuckyMist cried.

I heard arrows hitting her shield—the shield she picked up from her dead mate, Xenocide99.

Looking around frantically, I realized that I could still save them if I *focused*. I could defeat the Skeleton King!

I am ninja...

Zip.

Appearing in the middle of a group of skeletons firing on LuckyMist, I exploded into action, and destroyed them *all*...

Zip.

I warped next to trio of skeletons close together. They spread out quickly to flank me.

Zip, zip, zip.

I teleported back and forth between them, landing fierce blows that would have made my master proud, pounding them into dust!

Thunk.

Pain wracked my body again as an arrow hit me in the back!

I heard the low, violent *twang* of the Skeleton King's large bow, and looked up just in time to see a huge, black arrow fly across the courtyard ... and spear WolfBroJake in the leg!

The warrior cried out in pain, falling to a knee. He held up his shield as a volley of arrows launched at him from the nearest group of skeleton archers. His shield took most of them. A couple of arrows made it through his defenses.

WolfBroJake grunted in pain and defiance, then died in a puff of smoke. His gear fell to the ground.

The Skeleton King laughed again, his low chuckle echoing through the courtyard.

Zip.

I teleported to stand next to LuckyMist, and sent a palm strike into the face of the nearest approaching skeleton. Its helmet flew off and fell to the ground, and the undead archer burst into flames, unprotected in the daylight.

"STOP!!" the Skeleton King yelled, his voice booming.

I suddenly realized that we were completely surrounded. At least half of the skeleton army still remained. And the courtyard was littered with the bones of dozens and dozens of destroyed undead archers. Wooden bows and arrows were scattered around on the ground, and in *two distinct places* lay piles of Minecraftian gear...

Poor Xenocide99 and WolfBroJake.

Where would they reappear?

LuckyMist stood next to me, holding a battered sword and a shield bristling with arrows. Her armor was almost destroyed, and she was severely wounded.

The army of skeletons still had their bows aimed at us, and were hustling with small steps, reforming their position around us, until we found ourselves surrounded by a ring of undead.

Inside the ring of skeletons, LuckyMist and I stood on one side, and the Skeleton King stood on the other...

"An Enderman Ninja!" The Skeleton King bellowed. "Now I've seen everything!"

I could teleport away right now. I could flee this battle. But I would be abandoning LuckyMist to her death.

And a *real warrior* never flees from battle...

I clinched my large, black fists.

Pulled one of the arrows out of my body.

This battle could still be won. The Skeleton King was no match for *me*...

"Where is the beacon?" the Skeleton King yelled, his red eyes flaring in anger.

Now that the battle had quieted down, I could feel my *Chi* more clearly.

My pearl ... was almost *exhausted*.

Reaching out with my *Chi*, I felt for the Skeleton King's mind. I could sense the curse, the alien presence that didn't belong in our world. Tremendous *red energy*—loud and ugly. And the strangest thing? There was something about the monster's energy that was *different* in a way I hadn't felt before. It was like there were *two* entities, *together*, bound up tight inside the

208

monster's *Chi*—something small and strong and intelligent, and something huge and full of spikes and claws and death...

"*You mean the light artifact?*" I asked into his mind, extending my *mind voice* so that LuckyMist could hear. "*The source of your power? I have it...*"

The Skeleton King stared at me with his red, glowing eyes for a moment, processing the fact that I just spoke to him in his head and thinking about...

Thinking about...

Too much red energy—I couldn't read him.

The abomination started to laugh, a low, rolling chuckle of amusement that grew louder and more obnoxious until it boomed across the castle grounds.

I felt my Enderman rage bubble up inside of me, and pushed it back down.

"Silly Enderman," the Skeleton King said. "Ignorant fools. I would have expected more out of the Minecraftians, at least!" His voice was loud and low and rumbled through me. "That's not the *source of my power!* It was just a *beacon!* A magical *trinket* made from the heart of a demon that makes a pretty light and gives us some magical powers!"

The monster laughed.

"*Then what are you, abomination?*" I said into his mind.

"I am the Skeleton King!!" he bellowed. "And I will *rule* this world! Now give me back my beacon!"

"*Come and take it...*"

LuckyMist straightened and raised her shield. Terror came off of her in waves...

"Kill them!" the Skeleton King boomed.

All of the skeletons surrounding us suddenly drew and fired.

Zip.

Without thinking, I warped outside of the ring of archers, unharmed, but heard LuckyMist's scream as she was killed.

"*You monster!*" I yelled into the Skeleton King's mind. The Enderman rage *exploded* inside me like a burning fire!

Zip.

I warped back inside the ring as the skeletons fired again.

"Rrraaaarrr!" I roared as a couple of arrows pierced my body.

Zip.

I appeared in front of the Skeleton King, and exploded into action, landing a series of powerful strikes onto his massive, thick bony body. It was like hitting a stone wall. I remembered kicking his back.

Hearing the whistle of an arrow flying at me, I warped again to behind the abomination.

Zip.

Thunk.

I cried out in pain with my natural Enderman voice as another arrow hit me in the shoulder from somewhere else. Kicking out, I struck the Skeleton King in the back of the knee. He grunted in pain with his deep voice, and spun to face me.

"Cease fire!!" the Skeleton King roared, and all of the archers surrounding us lowered their bows.

"*I will defeat you and restore the balance, abomination...*" I said in his mind.

We began to circle each other.

The Skeleton King laughed. The skeleton archers all around us started stomping on the ground together, clattering their bones...

Clunk clunk clunk clunk clunk clunk clunk...

"So you think you can defeat *me*, huh?" the Skeleton King said. "You're not looking too hot, Enderman..."

"*You're not looking too good yourself, monster,*" I responded.

"Come at me then!!" the Skeleton King roared, then raised his great, black bow and fired.

I saw the large, black arrow coming at me for an instant, then warped out of the way.

Zip.

Appearing behind him, I launched into a flurry of powerful blows, my fists and feet crunching his massive, bony back. The monster spun around to face me.

Zip.

Behind him again, I sent a roundhouse kick into the knee I hit before, and felt the smash of bone beneath the blade of my feet.

"Arrrgg!" he cried with his deep voice, and spun to face me again.

Zip.

I teleported behind him again, but was shocked to see that he was already facing me. The

213

Skeleton King had anticipated my move, and spun to face where I was about to be. The monster swung out with a backhand, which crashed into my head and sent me sprawling.

Clunk clunk clunk clunk clunk clunk clunk.

The rhythm of the skeletons all clattering their bones together continued...

The Skeleton King raised his wicked-looking bow and aimed at me as I lay vulnerable on the ground.

I shook my head to clear the dizziness.

Found my *Chi*...

Zip.

I teleported behind him again, and sprang to my feet.

The Skeleton King turned before I was able to attack, and swung at me with a massive, bony fist.

Catching his large fist and redirecting his energy, I blocked the attack, then counter-attacked with a powerful kick that connected to his chest with a satisfying *crunch*.

The Skeleton King staggered back, then reeled, stunned from the blow...

"*I will end you, abomination,*" I said into his mind, then ran toward him as best I could with a hurt leg. Leaping into the air, I launched into another *flying dragon kick*, just like when I kicked him off the balcony...

Flying through the air, I visualized my kick hitting the Skeleton King in the center of his chest. I saw myself kicking *through* him, shattering the monster into many massive bones. I saw the Minecraftians, my friends, and thought about the abomination's bellowing laughter when they died...

My foot was justice. My attack was death.

I am the warping wind...

Then, just as my foot was about to connect, I was shocked when the Skeleton King's massive ribcage split apart up the center and *opened up* like a sideways chest—like a great clam-shell trap—and my body crumpled inside of it!

215

The ribcage *trap* slammed shut on me, crushing me inside of the abomination's body.

Pain...

I cried out, and roared in agony!

The Skeleton King's chest was large enough that such an attack would have totally swallowed up a Minecraftian. But I, as an Enderman, was too big to be completely enclosed, so I was tangled up in a deathtrap of bones, crushed, stuck...

Then, the ribcage opened up and spat me back out onto the ground.

I landed in the dirt, feeling broken.

Trying to get to my feet, I barely noticed the Skeleton King raise his bow to me again.

Zip.

I teleported just a few feet away as he fired, the black arrow hitting the ground where I was.

When I appeared, I collapsed onto the ground again.

Clunk clunk clunk clunk clunk clunk clunk.

I was exhausted and broken.

Where was my *Chi?*

It was gone … depleted…

Clunk clunk clunk clunk clunk clunk clunk.

The Skeleton King turned, and raised his bow again.

Fired.

I had nothing. My *Chi* was gone…

The black arrow pierced my chest and almost pinned me to the ground. The pain was unbelievable…

This was the end. I was done for.

I was wreckless.

Overconfident. I let my own ego defeat me…

I led the Minecraftians to their deaths, and killed myself with my own foolishness…

"Give me the beacon!" the Skeleton King roared.

I could barely see.

Clunk clunk clunk clunk clunk clunk clunk.

Looking up at him, I tried to get to my feet, then fell again.

In the haze of the pain, my master's voice came back to me again:

"The ultimate ninja does not rely on his hands or feet to defeat his opponent, but rather his mind..."

"Give me the beacon or DIE!!" the abomination bellowed.

Instead of trying to get back to my feet, I focused on ... sitting. Crossing my legs around the arrows sticking out of me, I tried to straighten my back...

"Last chance, Enderman!!" the Skeleton King said.

Clunk clunk clunk clunk clunk clunk clunk.

I knew he was aiming his bow at my head, but I wasn't looking at him.

I was looking at the roof above the balcony. I placed my hands above my knees, open to the *Chi* of the Overworld, waiting for the spark inside me to receive the power from the pearl seeds all around me. I could feel the seeds in the dirt under me, under the castle, in the hills of the forest...

It flowed into me.

Zip.

I was on the roof.

"What?!" the Skeleton King roared down below. "Where did he go?"

The rhythmic clunking of the skeletons' bones stopped as the army fanned out, looking for me everywhere.

I could barely feel my *Chi*. Whatever energy I absorbed from the world down there was almost gone again from that *one warp*.

Looking down into the shadowy section of the forest on the other side of the courtyard, I closed my eyes and meditated, letting go of my surrounding and the battle, trying to ignore the bellowing voice of the Skeleton King trying to find me...

I focused on my tiny spark of *Chi*.

Feeling the energy in the world around me, I tried to coax the spark into a small flame...

Tink.

A single arrow glanced off of the wall near me and fell back down to the ground. A skeleton had spotted me and missed.

"There he is!! FIRE!"

I heard the twangs of many bows and the whistling of a volley of arrows in the air.

Zip.

Trying to get to my feet, I looked behind me and saw the skeleton army firing dozens of arrows at my previous position. The Skeleton King and his minions all looked around in different directions trying to spot me. Several undead archers saw the purple motes of light drifting down through the air from my *warp pattern*, and started heading my way.

I limped off into the darkness of the forest, trying to stay in the shadows. I had to buy myself some time to recharge my *Chi*. A chase like this could go on forever—I would never be able to get ahead enough to warp back to The End if I kept having to make little jumps like this to get away!

I had no idea how many arrows were sticking out of me—I'd lost track. And the large, black arrow hurt the most...

Almost *Chi* enough to warp again...

"There he is!" the Skeleton King roared.

I was being pursued by the entire army—or what was left of it.

There was *no way* I was going to win this fight today...

Arrows started hitting the trees around me. Soon, they would catch up.

I sat again, a pine tree to my back, and pulled the *Chi* out of the ground...

Zip.

Appearing at the top of the tree, I sat in the sunshine and meditated.

"Up in the tree!" the Skeleton King yelled, his booming voice closer now.

My *Chi* was a little stronger now! A little more than a spark, but just one warp away from being depleted again if I wasn't careful. I would wait as long as I could...

The daylight shined in my face and the wind blew the tails of my headband around my shoulders as I let the energy of the Overworld flow into me. The army of Skeletons milled around below, shooting arrows into the air ineffectively. The closest arrows lost themselves in the boughs and branches.

"Come down, Ninja, and we'll kill you quickly!!" the Skeleton King roared. He was right below me.

Soon after, I felt the tree start shaking as the abomination punched it with his massive fists again and again.

That was enough…

I pulled out my compass and looked to the *north*. Somewhere, over there, not far, was the Minecraftians' dirt cave. I could hide out there until I could revive enough *Chi* to teleport back to my world…

Zip, Zip.

I teleported to the farthest treetop I could manage, then did it again.

My *Chi* was almost gone again.

Looking down to the shadowy forest floor, I dropped down as carefully as I could, and grunted when it still hurt a lot on my wounded leg.

The army was far behind me now, but if I was reckless again, that could change in a hurry. I had to stay ahead of them…

Limping through the shadows of the pine trees, I frequently checked my compass, and kept heading north. With my *Chi* low, I decided to wait until I needed it for an emergency, and continued on foot.

Behind me, not far, I heard the clattering of bones, and the repeated bellows of the Skeleton King.

"Find him!! Find the Enderman!"

After what seemed like an eternity of being pursued, I finally saw something I recognized...

Boot Rock!

At last! The cave! Scouring the area for the small hole I was looking for as the army advanced on me, I eventually found it—stacked blocked of dirt that looked meant to hold a door!

The last time I was outside this little dirt dwelling, I realized that I would have to *crawl* to get inside.

I never thought I'd actually *have* to.

Crawling carefully, grimacing at the pain of the arrows in my body, I pulled myself into the hole, then pulled a few dirt blocks out of the floor, and entombed myself into darkness.

Dragging myself to the middle of the small, bare dirt room, I pulled my broken body back into a sitting position again, and began to meditate.

With the limited amount of *Chi* I had, I could sense the skeleton archers swarming around outside on the surface, looking for me, as well as the huge, red ball of negative energy that was the Skeleton King, stomping around up there...

Despite the pain, I closed my eyes, slowed my breathing, and focused on the *Chi* of the world.

After a long time sitting in the darkness, surrounded by my enemies who wanted to kill me, I grew my *Chi* little by little, back into a powerful force of wisdom again...

And I warped back to *The End*.

Day 11 – The End

Defeat.

I felt the crushing weight of defeat.

The void swam over me, and normal Enderman walked about tending to their business, looking at my broken body with curiosity.

Eventually, I was able to pull out all of the arrows, including the large, black arrow that skewered my torso. My black blood ran from my wounds until I was able to stop the flow with my *Chi*.

When I had the energy, I would teleport across the void to the temple of the *Order of the Warping Fist* on the outer rim.

I sat on the dragon's island and meditated, trying to build up my *Chi* as other Endermen walked and warped around me.

Thinking back to when I was a youngling beginning the rigors of *initiate training*, I remembered my fight with Edon, another ninja

227

initiate in my class—the last time I suffered defeat. In a tournament of skill, small younglings testing their budding might against other small younglings, I *knew* that I was the superior fighter, matched up against Edon.

But young Edon knew that too, and he goaded me into flaunting my superior martial skills. Once I started over-extending myself, and leaving myself vulnerable out of *ego*, he closed in and beat me...

My master had told me, "*Do not confuse the voice of ego with that of intuition.*"

My ego defeated me then. And it defeated me again today.

Master Ee'char had also told me, "*In battle, your opponent is the teacher, and your ego is the enemy...*"

I never thought anything more of that lesson, until today.

I *failed* my lesson from the Skeleton King...

And now, I would have to explain to my master that I had failed in my mission as well.

But I wasn't finished.

Thinking about the village, I hoped that the Skeleton King wouldn't decide to attack the community. Why would he? He didn't know the villagers had helped us. Unless he figured it out somehow...

Unless he found one of the Minecraftians, and followed them back to the village.

That's what I would do...

And where were the Minecraftians now?

I was pretty sure that they needed their beds to control their location of regeneration, and I didn't remember seeing any new beds in their house in the village.

When they were killed, did they just respawn in a random place with nothing but the clothes on their backs? Were they together again by now? Or was LuckyMist running from the

Skeleton King's archers somewhere in the forest, unarmed and defenseless?

They had lost all of their weapons and armor, and there was no iron back in the village for them to make more equipment!

I had failed them...

I was *so sure* that we could defeat the army without trouble, that I led them straight to their deaths. My *Chi* had picked up on their energy, on their *feelings*, and I knew beyond the shadow of a doubt that they had *believed* in me. They put their lives ... into my hands.

Lifting my bloodied hands up before me, I flexed my long, slender fingers in the dim light of my home world. I heard the creaking of the dragon's wings as it flew by, near me. Clenching those long, black fingers into fists, I teleported to the Temple.

I would not fail again.

I would not fail my friends!

Pulling the compass from my pack, I stared at the red needle, and the red letter *N*—an odd color that stood out on this world.

I needed to work with my master, and learn the *Chi Dodge*.

No more *winging* it.

The true work of the martial arts is progress, not perfection.

Once my body was healed, and my *Chi* was full again, I would return to *Nexus 426* and help the Minecraftians reclaim their home.

We would try again, and we would win!

And I would be guided by my *Chi* and my mind—*not* by my ego.

I would restore the *balance*.

Looking at the purpur bridge to the Temple, I recalled the middle ninja that had been sitting there a few days ago, meditating and healing his wounds from the Overworld.

Putting the compass into my dimensional pocket, I walked across the bridge, and entered the Temple...

I would return...

Box Set Book 3:
Diary of an Enderman Ninja

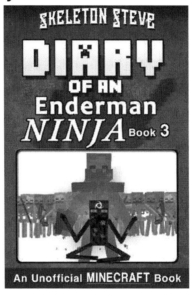

Elias the Enderman Ninja must redeem himself!

After suffering defeat in Book 2 by letting his ego lead the battle against the Skeleton King, Elias and the three Minecraftians are scattered and downtrodden. While healing his broken body in The End, Elias decides to return to Nexus 426 after some training with his master, to rejoin his friends and finish the battle he started...

This time, they'll do it right.

But will an Enderman initiate ninja and three rough-and-tumble Minecraftians, even with their new resolve and the power of the Beacon, be able to defeat such a strong adversary?

Day 12 – The End

The void swam over me.

Black and shades of purple, glittering with a million points of dim light, the expanse of nothingness swirled and sank, rose and shifted, ever moving, always as if alive but … nothing.

Even with my eyes closed, I could *feel* it all around me. Pushing in on me, but pulling away.

It was nothing.

The *great* nothing.

And I, an Enderman ninja, was nothing beneath it. Above it.

The empty sea of nothing surrounded me…

My pearl was warm, and my *Chi* was reaching out to the void around me like an exploding star…

Sitting with my back straight and my hands open, palms up on my knees, open to the void and the simplicity of *The End*, I meditated, focusing on

235

repairing my body. I encouraged my *Chi* to mend the multiple arrow wounds I suffered at the hands of the Skeleton King and his army.

The hundred or so undead archers had struck me a dozen times. I didn't even bother *counting* the arrows I pulled from my broken form yesterday. And the Skeleton King, himself, had skewered me with a long, black bolt that was more like a *spear* than an arrow...

The same big, black arrow he used to kill Xenocide99.

And again to mortally wound WolfBroJake, before the great Minecraftian warrior succumbed to the archers around him...

Dark thoughts bounced around in my head.

I let the thoughts all go, and they drifted off into the void...

The End was empty of *Chi* other than the energy *we Ender* brought back with us from the Overworld, as well as the *pearls* within each of us.

From far away—far, far away—I could sense the huge mass of *Chi* emanating from the dragon's island, from the *thousands* of pearl seeds growing in the endstone. Even though I could not see the island from this distance with my eyes, my *Chi* detected it like a blazing sun. And all of the Endermen spaced throughout the outer islands, each holding their *own* pearls and *Chi* within their individual bodies, were like *stars* in the darkness around me.

When I returned here, narrowly escaping the Skeleton King's army with my life, I was so broken up and wounded that I could hardly move.

And when I finally had the strength to teleport to the outer islands, to return to the Temple and report to my master that I had *failed* … he said nothing.

Master Ee'char merely sent me out here to heal…

"*Come back when you have regenerated your body, initiate, and we will discuss your mission,*" he had told me, short and to the point.

So for several hours now, I've been sitting and meditating on my own tiny island out in the void, surrounded by hundreds of other small, uninhabited isles.

Rocks floating through space.

The tall, slender chorus fruit trees stood quiet and waved slightly in the darkness, moving from time to time in the astral winds that barely blew, like long, purple fingers reaching up into the void.

Failure.

Defeat.

My spirit was crushed. Just like *that*, when I realized my error, the battle was lost and all I could do was try to escape—to do what I could to redeem myself and live to fight another day...

I thought of LuckyMist.

And Xenocide99, and WolfBroJake.

I had failed them.

In my arrogance, listening more to my ego than my good sense and strategic skills, I had let my friends down, and now they were dead.

Respawned, I thought.

Minecraftians don't die. They respawn.

But now, I didn't even know where they were or what they were doing. They were probably separated, and had lost all of their weapons, gear, and armor.

Even though I was fairly unfamiliar with Minecraftian customs and technology, I remembered what they said. Because I had managed to gather a lot of food for them from their farm and kitchen during my *scouting mission* of the castle before the attack, I knew that they wouldn't be hungry … assuming that they made it back to the village.

But I knew that they needed more *iron* to make weapons, tools, and armor. Iron that *they* and the *village* didn't have…

The Minecraftians had put all of their faith into me and my plan to attack the Skeleton King. And they all died—I hardly made it out alive.

They would not put their faith in me again...

If I was to return to the Overworld, to complete my mission and somehow defeat the Skeleton King, I could not expect them to follow me.

Not *another* time.

The End was simple and mostly devoid of energy. It was comfortable, with little to distract my mind.

As I sat straight, meditating, willing my wounds to mend, there weren't many sounds around me. Sometimes, I heard the *zip* of an Enderman passing by.

But I was mostly alone.

Just me ... and my island...

I knew that I was strong, and could be a force to be reckoned with. But how did I become so *blind?* How did I ever allow my *ego* to take over?

On the Overworld, I was among the most powerful of creatures existing there.

Here, on The End, I was a member of the *Order*, stronger than most of my race, but still *just another Enderman*. And there were many Endermen here far stronger than me.

And then there was the dragon...

My personal strength must have gone to my head after I defeated the Minecraftians, back before I even learned of the Skeleton King.

Walking the areas around *Nexus 426*, I was like a *god* among all of the natural mobs and animals. And then, when I proved myself stronger than the three Minecraftians living there?

Yes, I thought. *That's what happened*.

Moving on to our mission, being treated like heroes by the villagers, being looked up to as the Minecraftians' leader, I had felt *unstoppable*.

And I let it go straight to my head!

What was an army of just a hundred or so armored skeletons, boosted by the powers of the

241

beacon? What was a towering, intelligent abomination *Skeleton General* with a magic bow?

What a fool I was...

Yes, stealing the beacon during the beginning of the battle was a good move. Eventually, the beacon's magic wore off of the skeleton army.

But my plan, my strategy, was *thin* and reckless.

I should have taken more time to think. I should have made plans to divide the Skeleton King's forces, or to force them into some sort of bottleneck—anything to make the Minecraftians' job in the battle easier ... and safer.

Instead, I threw them to the wolves, expecting that nothing would go wrong.

Sitting straight with my hands unmoving on my knees, my *Chi* rolled and boiled around me, pulling my skin and insides back together.

And I shook my head in shame...

Day 13 – The End

After a while, when I felt close to fully-healed, I stood, perched on the top of my small island, floating through the void.

Opening my eyes, the dim and subtle purple colors of the nothingness around me helped to relieve the pain I felt in my soul. I warped from island to island, back to the Temple.

Zip.

Walking through the entryway on the other side of the long purpur bridge, I warped up the central tower to the main dojo, where my master would likely be waiting for me up on the roof.

Stepping into the dojo, I was surprised to see that it was dark, and empty.

Usually, the dojo was full of youngling initiates taking lessons from the master-level ninjas.

Now, there was *nothing*, and I scanned the vast, empty space with eyes and my *Chi*.

243

Suddenly, I startled when I heard the sound of a *fireball* sizzling through the darkness.

Boom!

A ball of energy that glowed like lava crashed into my left side, and the explosion threw me to the ground. The stone floor of the dojo was jarring, and in that moment, I felt the same *smack* of my head hitting the hard purpur surface as I felt countless times growing up...

Leaping to my feet and clearing my head, I looked at all corners of the room, and saw nothing but darkness. Reaching out with my *Chi*, I could feel that the nearest Endermen were several islands away...

The Temple—*empty?*

Another fireball appeared from a dark corner to my right, and I saw it in time, speeding at me across the room.

Zip.

Warping out of the way, I saw it *crash* into the wall on the opposite side of the dojo.

244

The explosion didn't harm any of the martial arts training equipment that lined the sides of the room.

They would only harm *me*...

A third fireball suddenly bolted at me from behind. I couldn't hear it, but I could *almost* sense it coming. Turning to see it, I watched for a split-second as the sphere of deadly energy flew at me with great speed...

Zip.

I teleported out of the way...

Boom!

A fourth fireball exploded into my back, making me grunt in my natural Enderman voice, and throwing me onto the floor.

My chest and face impacted the purple stone with a sharp pain.

"Grrrrrrr..." I growled with my natural voice and jumped to my feet.

"*Why are you still weak with your Chi Dodge, initiate?*" Master Ee'char's voice boomed inside my head. "*Why do you not dodge like an Ender??*"

I shook my head violently to clear out the pain from hitting my face on the floor.

Darkness. I still couldn't see him...

"*I don't know, master!*" I responded with the *mind voice*. "*I have not yet mastered the Chi Dodge...*"

Another fireball appeared from the darkness, speeding at my head, glowing and leaving a trail of smoke behind it.

Zip.

Boom!

Warping out of the way of the one I saw coming at me, I landed right in the path of another I didn't see. The explosion knocked me to the ground.

I spit some of my black blood out onto the purpur floor.

My master was anticipating my warps, and I could only dodge what I could see coming!

"You came back to me, retreating from your mission, full of arrows!" he said, his voice loud and as clear as a bell in my mind. *"How embarrassing..."*

I suddenly saw the glow of green eyes emerge from the darkness.

Spinning to face him, I readied myself to dodge another fireball...

But he only stepped out from the shadows, his hands down, his face disappointed.

"My master," I said into his mind, dropping to my knees. *"I am sorry ... I just ... I haven't figured out..."*

"Initiate Elias," he said. *"I have already given you the key."*

"But I'm trying, master," I said. *"I dodge many, but I can't dodge them all..."*

"You didn't dodge enough, young one," he responded. *"And you should not be trying! Do not*

learn to try harder. Instead, the key is to learn how not to try in the first place..."

"*I do not understand,*" I said.

"*You will,*" he said. "*You must.*"

So we trained.

We trained for several hours.

I could always dodge out of the way of the fireballs when I saw them coming, just like I had with the arrows from the undead archers. But when my master launched his *Chi* projectiles at me when I didn't *see* them, and I didn't have time to react ... I got the chance to taste the dojo floor again.

Eventually, Master Ee'char was fed up with my reliance upon *trying*, and instructed me to blindfold myself with my blue *initiate rank* headband.

I moved the headband down over my eyes, and found that I was rather *helpless* against the silent fireballs. Without my eyes and ears to guide me, I took blow after blow, only managing to dodge here and there, out of luck or...

There was something—a little *spark* of something—that I couldn't quite put my finger on. A little thing inside that told me that the fireball was coming...

But it was a very small, very *quiet* thing, and I could barely hear it...

"*Do!*" Master shouted into my mind. "*Do! Do not try. You must do!*"

We eventually stopped and walked up the stairs to the roof of the dojo as younglings and their teachers filed back into the building.

Sitting together near Master Ee'char's many potted plants from the Overworld, we meditated for a while together.

"*Initiate Elias,*" my master said. "*Your head and body are still not one.*"

"*How do I fix it, master?*" I asked.

"You must listen. Become one with your Chi. Only when you let your Chi move you, and stop moving yourself, will you master the Chi Dodge…"

Day 14 – The End

Master Ee'char and I meditated together for a long while up on the roof of the *Order's* main dojo.

Eventually, we spoke more, and I told him all about my experiences on Overworld surrounding *Nexus 426* and my quest to restore the balance. I told him about the Minecraftians, and my initial battle with them, about learning of the Skeleton King, our journey to the village, my scouting of the castle, the beacon, the battle...

I also told him about the revelations I had about my *ego*, and the arrogance that blinded me and led to my defeat. We discussed the feelings and thoughts I experienced while meditating and healing alone out on the small, remote island.

"It seems that you have learned from your own lessons about the danger of mixing ego with your martial arts," Master said in my mind.

"I wish I hadn't been so stupid!" I said.

"*Do not wish to change the past, initiate,*" my master said. "*Your folly led to unfortunate events and the suffering of you and your friends, but your mistakes can be your greatest teacher.*"

I contemplated that.

"*...Your greatest teacher since you survived, that is,*" he went on to say. Master Ee'char opened his ancient, glowing green eyes, and looked into mine. "*You are now well. You say that your Minecraftian comrades have regenerated somewhere, so they are well. This was a valuable lesson.*"

"*But they won't trust me now,*" I said. "*I failed them.*"

"*Then that is your next challenge. Do not fail them again,*" he responded. "*Master your Chi Dodge and succeed in your mission.*"

"*Can't I take other ninjas with me?*" I asked. "*This mission would be easy to complete if I and several other ninjas worked together. We could destroy the army in no time, and restore the balance!*"

"*No, initiate*," Master Ee'char said. His spirit felt like a tower of strength, and I knew that there would be no arguing with him. "*This is your mission. You pass or fail by your own strength, by your own wits and resources, by your own skills and Chi...*"

"*Yes, master,*" I said.

I thought about asking if my success in this mission would warrant my promotion to the rank of lower ninja. But I decided against it.

Such thoughts got me into this mess in the first place...

It was my duty as a member of the *Order of the Warping Fist* to maintain the balance of Overworld for the success of the Ender race!

I am ninja.

Other Endermen had little in the way of duty—partake in the Seed Stride, protect the dragon.

But my *life* was duty to the Ender race.

253

Being so focused before on increasing my rank before made me lose sight of what was really important. I knew that if I performed my duty, and learned through the lessons of experience, that I would grow stronger, and my rank would increase naturally on its own...

This time, I'd do the mission for the right reasons.

I had to restore the balance and destroy the abomination. For *Overworld* and for the Ender race.

And I had to help my *friends*.

I wouldn't let them down again...

Opening my eyes, I saw my master sitting across from me, watching me, a faint smile on his face...

"*Initiate Elias,*" he said. "*I can sense your Chi growing in the right direction.*"

He stood, so I did as well.

"*Young one, focus on learning your Chi Dodge. That will lead you to victory. You must return to your mission. There is no more time for training. The balance must be restored!"*

I bowed.

"Yes, master."

Leaving the Temple and teleporting to the Hub, I focused on *Nexus 426*, and warped back to the *Overworld*...

Day 14 – Overworld

Appearing in the desert around *Nexus 426*, the sun was intense in the noon sky, and sand blew past me in gusts of wind.

Sure is bright, I thought, shielding my eyes until I adjusted to the white-hot light of the arid biome.

I don't know if I'd *ever* get used to how the daylight hurt my eyes. Maybe my fellow Endermen were right to stay out of the sun and only explore the Overworld at night.

But that didn't matter now.

I had a job to do.

Looking around the hot desert, I was reminded of when I first started my mission days ago. The same dense forest stood to the east, and a large grassland to the west.

If I didn't already know which way was which, I would have needed to use the *compass* that LuckyMist had given me, because the hot, square sun blazed at the very *top* of the sky.

To the south stood the imposing mountain of stone, where I had found the Minecraftians originally, back before I knew anything about the Skeleton King.

Zip.

Warping in short hops across the desert, I made my way to the mountain and the Minecraftians' old *cave home*.

I could at least start my journey there, and give my eyes a break from the sun in its deep shadows.

Eventually, I landed in the stone bowl of the cave's entrance. Thinking back to when I first saw the Minecraftians, I looked at the cobblestone walls of their cave home and LuckyMist's mine— the wooden doors they left in place, the torches on the walls, my perch up in the darkness of the cliff from where I watched them—

Wait—*torches?*

As I recalled, the Minecraftians took every scrap of their gear and stuff with them, with the exception of the doors.

So why were there *torches* on the walls?

Zip.

With a short teleport, I appeared at the window of the cave home, and looked inside.

Crafting table. Furnace. A bed...

They were here! Or ... *someone* ... was here!

I looked over the wooden door.

How *did* they open these doors? What trick did the Minecraftians perform to get them to *pop* open like that? I pressed on its surface. Tapped the four corners. Tried to slide it.

No luck.

Walking back out into the bowl of the cave entrance, I sat on the raw stone floor in the same place I sat fairly recently, straightening my back, and crossed my legs. Putting my hands, palms up, on my knees, I closed my eyes and extended my *Chi* into the area around me...

No energy. Nothing.

Attuning myself to the dormant *pearl seeds* hiding in the dirt blocks below me and in the mountain, I opened myself up to the *Chi* of the Overworld around me. I tried to listen farther...

There was something ... some small energy—urgent, bright and determined—down below in the mine...

I waited.

The sun traveled across the desert sky, making its way toward the grassy plains until late afternoon rolled around.

Eventually, the door to the mine popped open.

It was LuckyMist!

She was surprised to see me.

"Elias!" she cried, running over and grabbing my sitting form in a weird Minecraftian ritual—a *hug*...

I'd seen her share these 'hugs' with Xenocide99 several times.

"*Hello, LuckyMist,*" I said into her mind. "*It is good to see you alive.*"

Her cheerful attitude was diminished suddenly, and she looked down to the ground, but recovered quickly and smiled at me again.

"You too! You're *alive!!*"

"Where are the others?" I asked. "Are they okay?"

LuckyMist composed herself and closed the door to the mine. She looked out to the forest in the east.

"Yeah ... they're okay, I guess. They're back at the village—waiting for *you*, actually!"

"*What are you doing here at the cave?*" I asked.

She wasn't wearing any armor. Her pink and blue clothes was bright and bold in the sun. In her hand was a pickaxe—not made from iron like the tools she typically used. This one was crude, and made from stone.

"I uh …" she stammered. I could sense that she was flustered, and feeling unsure of herself. "We … after we … *died* … we were—oh man, that was terrible! What a *horrible* battle. How did you survive? When they killed me, I respawned in the forest, and just *ran and ran and ran*. I was sure they killed *you* too…"

I stood, and extended my long arm to put a hand on her shoulder, mimicking a Minecraftian gesture I'd seen several times now. My long fingers wrapped around her diminutive form. Minecraftians were so small…

"I almost died too, LuckyMist," I said in her mind. *"After you were killed, I fought the Skeleton King in personal combat. He—"*

"Ohmygod, you did? You went *toe to toe* with that monster? What happened??"

I remembered suddenly how the Skeleton King's ribcage opened like a sideways bear-trap and … *caught* me … in the middle of my kick. I remembered how he almost pinned me to the ground like a bug with his wicked, black bow…

"*I was defeated, LuckyMist*," I said. "*I narrowly escaped with my life*."

"I'm glad," she said quietly, then looked up suddenly. "Glad that you *escaped*, that is. You got away…"

"*Yes*," I said.

I thought about everything I wanted to tell her—about how sorry I was for bringing them into danger with a reckless plan of attack. About how bad I felt for letting them down when they looked up to me to *lead* them, and put their faith in me completely. They trusted in my judgment, and they did everything I told them too…

And I got them killed.

The thoughts were at the front of my mind. The apology…

But I couldn't say it.

"The others are in the village," she said. "We didn't know if you were dead or what, so they wanted to wait for you there. I tried to convince them to just come back here with me, but they wouldn't. Xenocide99 and I had a fight about it and ... I'm sorry," she said, laughing suddenly. "They're hoping you come back, and they want to go again—to kill the monster."

"*Why are you here?*" I asked again.

She looked down. "I just ... I couldn't stay. Another bunch of skeletons came to the village and took their iron and stuff, and I just didn't want to *deal* with that anymore." She cleared her throat and tossed her hair, looking up at my face. "So I came here. To start over. To have a quiet, little life, mining, and I'll build a new castle *somewhere else*."

"*We need to go back,*" I said. "*It is my duty to restore the balance—I must. We must try again. I know that I can succeed this time. We'll kill the Skeleton King and get your castle back!*"

LuckyMist's face paled, and she looked away.

"I ... I can't," she said.

"*I need your help, LuckyMist*," I said in her mind.

The Minecraftian female broke away from my gentle grip on her shoulder.

"No, Elias," she said. "I don't want to fight. I can't go back there."

"*LuckyMist*," I said. She didn't understand. "*This time we have the beacon, and...*"

Things are different, I wanted to say. I would be more careful. I'd think things through better, and not just have us go charging in...

"I can't!" she shouted. "I don't want to see that again!"

LuckyMist turned away from me, and walked to the entrance of the cave home. She stopped, then faced me again.

"I can help a little, I guess. I won't help you *fight*, but I can give you *this* to help the others." She opened the door and went inside. I heard the creak of a chest, and she stepped out again, offering me several handfuls of white, fluffy organic material. "I found some sheep in the forest there, and made myself a new bed. Take this wool, and give it to the others, and they can make beds too."

She held out her hand, offering the wool, and broke eye contact, looking at the stone ground.

We stood in silence for a while, me trying to think of another way to convince her. My *Chi* picked up on her energy, revealing that now, she really just wanted me to go away...

Reaching out, I took the wool, putting it into my dimensional pocket.

"*Thank you, LuckyMist,*" I said. "*I'll let Xenocide99 and WolfBroJake know that you're well.*"

She nodded, still looking at the ground, and made a small, private cry.

"Bye, Elias. Good luck," she said, then turned and disappeared inside.

Fear. Sadness. I sensed those slow, numbing emotions with my *Chi*.

LuckyMist had made her decision. Hopefully I could change her mind later.

One way or another, I would make it up to her, for letting her *down* before...

Turning back to the darkening sky, I warped around to the back of the mountain with a few short teleports.

Zip.

Pulling out the compass she gave me, I checked my heading, then started the journey *south* to the village. Mostly teleporting, I walked at times, and occasionally stopped to meditate and recharge my *Chi*.

I made it to the village just before dawn.

Day 15 – Overworld

As the sun rose over the yellowish grass field, the light of dawn glittered on the windows of the village, and I paused to watch the cobblestone and wooden buildings brighten under the new day.

I watched the undead mobs catch on fire and burn to the ground.

Before long, the doors of the small town started to spring open, and the villagers rushed out of their homes to mill about in their strange, urgent energy.

Warping into the middle of the village, I walked down the cobblestone streets to the house that the Minecraftians had chosen as their *temporary base* for our failed attack.

I heard the voices of the two Minecraftian males before they stepped outside.

"All in all, once this whole thing blows over, she's gonna be mad that you used up all the *leather*," WolfBroJake's voice said.

"Hey, *we* need it a lot more than some future plans of an *enchanting area*," Xenocide99 said. "We can always kill more cows."

"That's a *lot* of cows," WolfBroJake said.

"Big deal. We'll get the castle back eventually, then we can breed a *ton* of them. And I'll be happy to eat lots of *steaks* for a while. I'm getting tired of *pork chops*."

The door of their house popped open as I approached.

The two Minecraftian males ran out into the street. Xenocide99 was still dressed in his normal green shirt, and WolfBroJake in all black, but now they were both decked out in full suits of armor made from animal skins.

Leather, as they called it.

In WolfBroJake's hand was a crude sword made from a stick and a chunk of shaped stone, and Xenocide99 held a crude stone pick axe just like the one LuckyMist had.

When they saw me, their eyes widened and their mouths dropped open.

They glanced immediately at my headband, and knew it was me. If it wasn't for my *Order* rank headband, I would have looked like any other normal Enderman.

"*Hello, Minecraftians*," I said into their minds. "*I have returned.*"

"Holy cow!!" Xenocide99 said. "It's the *Enderman!*"

"You're back!" WolfBroJake exclaimed. He smiled. "I *knew* you'd be back!"

My *Chi* picked up on a sense of surprise and relief in their energy, and I felt a sort of … *affection* coming off of them. WolfBroJake moved like he was going to approach and maybe clap me on the arm, but he stopped himself, unsure.

"*Yes*," I said. "*I had to return to my world for a time to heal my body.*"

"Oh man," Xenocide99 said. "LuckyMist told us what happened to you guys after *we* died—how you got caught in a *ring* of them like that? Like he was setting you up to have a *duel* or something!"

"Oh yeah," WolfBroJake said, grinning. "That's *crazy*. Sounds intense!"

"*It was intense*," I said. "*We were defeated. I nearly perished.*"

"Dude..." WolfBroJake said. "What happened? I mean—after LuckyMist died? What happened to *you?*"

"*The Skeleton King and I fought in mortal combat. We were surrounded by the army as they made a sort of ... war rhythm with their bones...*"

"*Dude!*" Xenocide99 said. "That's awesome!"

How could these Minecraftians be so casual about a life and death struggle of such magnitude? They, themselves, died as well...

Because they always come back, I thought.

Death loses its meaning, loses its severity, when you can just *respawn* after being killed...

The thought of these two Minecraftians' casual approach to their *own deaths* lightened the load on my spirit a little, but I still felt bad about LuckyMist.

"Then what??" WolfBroJake asked.

"*We battled. At one point I thought I had the upper hand, but the Skeleton King had a few surprise moves of his own,*" I said into their minds. "*When the fight turned against me, he shot me with his bow, just as he did to the two of you. I tried to last as long as I could, and eventually escaped.*"

"Heavy..." Xenocide99 said. "What do you mean he *shot* you? Why didn't you just teleport out of the way?"

"Did your *Chi Dodge* let you down?" WolfBroJake asked.

Xenocide99 looked at him. "Yeah, he had *lots* of arrows sticking out of him by the time LuckyMist died, she said."

"*My Chi Dodge,*" I said, "*is still something I have to master.*" I instinctively reached to the scar on my chest where the huge, black bolt had speared through me and almost fastened me to the ground. "*I was unable to teleport anymore by then—I was exhausted...*"

We all stood quiet for a moment.

"Well, at any rate," WolfBroJake said, "I'm glad you're okay."

"Yeah, me too," Xenocide99 said. "You have a good plan?"

Plan?

That shocked me.

After my carelessness, after I led the Minecraftians into battle with an unclear mind, they were ready to take orders from me *again?*

"*Not yet*," I said.

"We don't really have the *gear* yet to launch another assault like that," WolfBroJake said. "We've been trying to find some iron, mining into the hills surrounding this place."

"Yeah, that's where we were about to go," Xenocide99 said. "Going back to go mine some more..."

"That reminds me," I said into their minds. *"I met up with LuckyMist yesterday back at your cave house, and she gave me this wool to give to you—for beds."*

Their eyes lit up at that.

Reaching into my dimensional pocket, I pulled out the six blocks of fluffy material, and handed them over.

"Thanks!" said WolfBroJake. "That's great!"

They took the wool, split it up, then ran back inside.

After a few minutes at the crafting table, they each put down a new, red-blanketed bed in opposite corners of the house. Stepping back outside again, the three of us chatted some more for a while, then WolfBroJake and Xenocide99 left to go mining for the day.

As the day went on, and the sun traveled through the sky, I warped around the village, stopping here and there to think.

We would need a superior strategy...

If we were to attack the Skeleton King again, without LuckyMist, without enough iron for the Minecraftians to have their best technology for battle, I would need to approach the attack *very carefully*.

The villagers bustled around town tending to their business, working their farm plots, processing animals for leather and meat, trading with each other—I could see that they were still *wary* of me, but no longer reeked of fear.

I found Kumara, the apprentice blacksmith, directing a couple of villagers who seemed to be the town's miners. Their energy was frantic and confused...

"*What is it, Kumara?*" I asked into his mind.

The blacksmith was surprised to see me. "*You have returned, Dark One!*" he said. "*We feared you were killed by the undead army!*"

I shook my head. "*I live, young villager. Now, what is wrong?*"

He looked at his miners, who looked at each other, then at me.

"*I fear that the army may return soon, Dark One, and they will be seeking more iron, but our ore vein has run dry, and we have little to give them...*"

I nodded, and walked on through the village, looking over each of the different buildings.

I had to come up with an idea...

Would the skeletons even return here? I thought. Probably. If the Skeleton King didn't believe the village to be involved in our failed attack before, there was no reason why he wouldn't continue extorting iron, and whatever other resources he wanted, from this place.

One of the village's buildings contained scores of books, and a female villager in white robes looked at my tall, black form through the window with wide eyes.

"*Greetings, villager.*" Pushing through a mental mess of fear in the villager's mind, I reached out with my *Chi* and asked, "*What is this place?*"

Taking her hands out of her robes in a flash, the villager in white robes pressed her palms against her head and closed her eyes, as if my words hurt her mind. Slowly, she looked up again, and opened her eyes.

"What is this?" she thought. "Are you speaking in my head?!"

"*I am,*" I responded in her mind. "*May I ask you some questions, villager? What is this place? Why do you have so many books?*"

Wary, eyes narrowed, she lowered her hands from her head, and folded them together under her robes again.

"*This is the village library, Ender,*" she said.

"*Are you familiar with the Ender race, librarian?*" I asked.

"*I have never met an Enderman,*" she responded in her mind, watching me through the window. "*But I have read about them here.*"

I looked down at the door to the library. The wooden piece of Minecraftian technology was just like the doors back at the cave home. How did these things open?? If this villager had learned about the Ender through the books stored in this building, then perhaps she could help me learn about the *beacon*...

"*May I enter, villager?*" I asked.

I could feel with my *Chi* that she was uncertain, but eventually moved to the door, and the wooden portal popped open.

Zip.

I warped inside through the open door, unable to bend far enough down to pass through without crawling.

The villager appeared surprised, but recovered quickly.

"What is the cloth band and symbol on your head?" she asked, looking up at me. I heard her thoughts clearly with my *mind voice*, but now that she was comfortable with such communication, the villager was also speaking with her natural voice at the same time.

I heard aloud, "Hmm .. Hurr ... hurrr?"

"It is the designation of my Order, and my rank within it," I said.

"What order is that?" she asked, moving to organize a collection of loose papers on a desk.

"The Order of the Warping Fist," I responded. *"The blue band I wear around my head is that of the initiate, and the symbol is the insignia of a Novice rank ninja."*

"That is interesting," she said, scrambling for a quill and ink. The villager began furiously scribbling down words on a page. *"What is the Order of the Warping Fist? I've never seen any reference to that anywhere in my books..."*

We spoke for a while about the Order. While my *Chi* detected her fear when she first saw me, now I was picking up solely the *urgent* energy that all of the villagers exhibited, and there was something else...

A vibrant *curiousity*...

"*Now that I have described to you many aspects of the Ender,*" I said into her mind, "*May I ask you something?*"

"*By all means,*" she replied, folding her hands into her white robes once again.

"*I was wondering if, with all of this information you have, in all of your books, if you could tell me about this?*"

I produced the *beacon* from my dimensional pocket. It was large, and cold, and glittered like crystal-clear ice in the afternoon sun that came in through the windows.

The villager's eyes widened in wonder...

"*I have not seen one of those before,*" she said in her mind. "*What is it?*"

"*I heard that it called a 'beacon'. It is an artifact that produces a brilliant light, and casts* magic over its allies. But I do not understand how it works…"

"I've never heard of a 'beacon' before," she said, looking it over. I had a feeling that if I placed it on the floor, it would cast its brilliant, evil red light up into the ceiling, even inside this place…

"Supposedly, it is made from the heart of a demon—whatever that means," I said.

"A demon, eh?" the librarian asked. "That sounds like the Nether."

The villager looked up at her shelves of books, then darted to one shelf in particular, pulled her hands out of her robes, and began rifling through the individual tomes.

"You are familiar with this … demon?" I asked.

She pulled one book, checked the cover, then pulled another.

"No," she said, "Not really—'demon' may just refer to the creatures that live in the Nether. But I do have a book about the Nether. I may be *able to find some information about it if you give me a little time..."*

"*Very well*," I said, putting the beacon back into my dimensional pocket. "*I'll return tomorrow.*"

I spent the rest of the evening walking the village, trying to think of a viable strategy for attacking the Skeleton King and his forces with a force even more weakened now than we were before.

Last time didn't work out so well...

Wracking my brain for clever strategies, I went over scenarios in my mind where we tried— the three of us—to use deception and trickery to somehow divide the forces into smaller groups. Or maybe, there might be a way to get the Skeleton King *alone*, so that we can attack him *together*...

But I couldn't think of anything solid.

Not yet.

I had a feeling that the beacon could be of great help if we could figure out how to use it—to take the power they used against us before, and turn it to work in our favor against *them*...

WolfBroJake and Xenocide99 returned before dark after a long day of not finding much iron.

By the time they returned, I could see that Xenocide99 now wore an iron helmet, and WolfBroJake had a shield and an iron sword, but still wore leather armor.

I told them about my conversation with the librarian, and Kumara's concern about the skeleton army returning any time now to steal more resources from the village. The two Minecraftians told me that, in the last few days, they had tried communicating with Kumara to work together to solve the iron situation, but without *my help*, they weren't able to understand each other, and all three ended up frustrated...

Day 16 – Overworld

After spending the night meditating on the roof of the Minecraftians' home, I was no closer to coming up with a viable strategy for attacking the Skeleton King again.

For a long part of the night, I contemplated the *Chi Dodge*, and tried for *hours* to feel the world around me with my *Chi*, to use my *Chi* as a reflex...

Without having my master's fireballs to practice with, I was unable to exercise my theories, or practice feeling anything coming at me without using my other senses.

In the morning, when the Minecraftians were awake, I approached Xenocide99.

"Good morning, ninja!" he said, putting together his mining gear for another day of work in the mines.

"*Yes it is, Xenocide99,*" I responded. "*Before you leave to seek more iron, I was wondering if you would be willing to help me with something...?*"

He looked over at WolfBroJake, then back at me.

"Of course, Enderman! What do you need?"

"*I admit,*" I said, "*that it feels strange to ask for … help … in this regard, but…*"

I hesitated.

Xenocide99 shook his head and smiled. "It's *fine*, dude. Whatever it is. What do you want me to do?"

"*I spent part of the night contemplating my Chi Dodge, and need to practice. But I'll need someone to … attack me, so that I may learn to react with my Chi.*"

Xenocide99 thought for a moment, running his hand through his hair.

"You want me to *shoot you?*"

"*Yes, Minecraftian. As I recall, you are very skilled with your bow. And I will require serious intent to harm in order to exercise my Chi…*"

He looked back to the house at WolfBroJake, who was leaning against the wall with his arms crossed, watching. The larger warrior nodded his head.

"Um, sure, I guess," Xenocide99 said. "But does it have to be *arrows?* I mean—I actually *got* you once before, and I don't want to *hurt* you. You know—in case the skeletons come back…"

"*What else did you have in mind?*" I asked in his mind.

"Well … we do have lots of *junk* inside from when you brought us food and other stuff from the castle before. There's also other small things we don't need. I have plenty of *ammo*—ink sacs, and spider eyes, and beet roots and such…"

I nodded.

"*I thank you for your assistance, Xenocide99,*" I said. "*Would you meet me in the field with said items?*"

The Minecraftian nodded, and disappeared back into the house. WolfBroJake followed.

Zip.

Teleporting out to the open grass field, just outside of the village, I waited for them to catch up.

For a while, I stood in the grass, and dodged as Xenocide99 threw objects at me. The Minecraftian throwing slow-moving *junk objects* at me wasn't nearly as effective as my master's *Chi* fireballs, likely not as effective as a fast-moving arrow, but it worked...

After successfully dodging several spider eyes, plant bulbs, and other small things the Minecraftians figured they didn't need, I stopped them long enough to move my headband down over my eyes.

To truly get in touch with my *Chi* defensively, I would have to be blindfolded...

Then ... the game became different.

Splat!

Something round and squishy struck my shoulder.

Standing still, reaching out with my *Chi*, I could detect the presence of Xenocide99 circling around me, and WolfBroJake watching from a short distance away. I could feel the presence of a few chickens in the field not far from us.

Thunk!

A small, hard object hit me in the chest.

But I could not detect the items flying at me through the air...

Eventually, WolfBroJake joined in, and they took turns throwing things at me from different directions.

Many small, roundish objects of various weight, hardness, and ... *squishiness* ... collided with my body, my arms and legs, my head. And just when I thought that this exercise was hopeless, I realized that I was starting to pick up on the *noise* in the *Chi* around me.

These objects were slower than an arrow or a fireball, and at times, I could just *barely feel* something in the air, like a tickle in the breeze, or a spot of color in darkness...

Zip.

"Holy cow!" Xenocide99 said. "You *did it!* You teleported out of the way of my beetroot!"

Thunk!

Then WolfBroJake hit me with a potato or something from the other side. I didn't feel it coming.

We practiced like that for another hour or so, as I reached out with my *Chi* and tried to listen to the smaller things in the energy field around me.

I may have successfully dodged out of the way of a handful more incoming objects, but mostly, I was just pelted *again and again* with ink sacs, spider eyes, and plants.

There was still a long way to go...

And we didn't have much time.

Later, after the two Minecraftians had left to continue their work in the mine, I returned to the librarian.

"*Have you learned more about the beacon?*" I asked in her mind, stooping below the ceiling inside the library.

"*Some,*" she responded, "*but nothing that would help you use it.*" The villager in white robes held a book up to me from the desk where she had been reading. With a squat, square finger, she pointed out a picture within its pages of a large, dark-grey monster, floating above a trail of smoke. Its body was amorphous, and it had three wicked skull-shaped heads atop broad shoulders. No arms or legs. "*This is a Wither,*" she said. "*It's a vicious and terrible beast of the Nether. According to my book, your 'beacon' is made from something called a Nether Star—the heart of this demon.*"

She lowered the book back to the desk.

"*That's interesting,*" I said, "*but I take it, despite this knowledge about where the beacon comes from, you didn't find anything about how to use it?*"

The librarian shook her head.

"It's a rare artifact, that beacon," she said. *"I doubt anyone here would be able to help you…"*

I thanked her and left, walking the village for a while, trying to come up with ideas to defeat the Skeleton King.

Later, there was a commotion at the blacksmith's.

The villagers hustled and bustled to Kumara's building, and the energy in the air was urgent and excited!

"What is it, Kumara?" I asked with my *mind voice*, as the apprentice blacksmith spoke in his villager language to a couple of farmers.

He turned to me, his eyes wide and beaming.

"Oh, Dark One, this is good!! Good news! My master, Balder, has returned!"

Just then, the older blacksmith, dressed in brown and black robes that were now tattered and dirty from days in the forest, stepped out into the forge area from inside the dwelling. The master

292

blacksmith's eyes widened when he saw me standing among the villagers next to his apprentice.

We stood, facing each other.

"Hurr," he said. "Hmm hurr…"

"*Enderman*," his thoughts said as he spoke. "*It pleases me to see you here…*"

I bowed.

"*Balder, master blacksmith*," I responded. "*It is good to see you as well, free and safe.*"

"*Free, thanks to you*," he said. "*I am in your debt for releasing me from the Skeleton King's prison.*"

"*How did you escape?*" I asked. "*We were defeated in the battle outside…*"

"*Just as you instructed me, Dark One*," he said. "*I hid in the farm until the undead were gone, then made my way home.*"

Young Kumara watched with rapt attention, even though he could only hear his master's words as he spoke aloud in the villager language. I extended my *Chi* to allow him to listen in on the conversation.

"*You left as the skeletons were battling us in the courtyard?*"

"*Yes, but I took something with me first,*" he said, smiling. "*I did not know the way the battle would go, so to ensure that the Skeleton King could not return to his former power, I took back all of the iron blocks that lay beneath the beacon…*"

That must have been what he was doing inside the blacksmith building—putting the blocks into the chest inside…

"*That is good news indeed,*" I said. "*But how did you escape the forest? There must have been at least fifty skeletons searching for me when I was trying to get away…*"

"*With this,*" he said. Balder pulled a small, round object, and a large, rolled-up scroll of paper, from his robes.

The small object was a compass, just like the one I had—a gift from LuckyMist.

"The Skeleton King did not know that I had a map. It is something that I always carry—I have for years."

The blacksmith unrolled the large piece of paper, and I looked in awe at a detailed drawing of what appeared to be this region, as seen from above. In the upper-central area of the paper, I saw a depiction of what must have been *this village*—I recognized the layout from all of the time I've spent on the roofs here in the last week. Far below the illustration of the village was a drawing of a castle, and a rendering of a forest of pine trees was drawn in between, in a vibrant, dark green.

And there was more than just the village, and the Minecraftians' castle, and the land between them. The map's drawings extended far to what must have been the *east* and *west*— though it was more elaborated to the east. My eyes scanned over colorful drawings of grasslands, rocky hills, even a *lake*, and what seemed to be another village near the eastern edge of the page...

I had never seen anything before like it.

"*Remarkable,*" I said into his mind. "*You have explored far around here...*"

"*Indeed,*" Balder responded. "*And that's how I returned. You're right—the Skeleton King had his entire army scouring the forest around the castle. They were difficult to evade. The undead were searching for you for a long time.*" He paused, and laughed. "*And I bet that they still are! You took his beacon—he is desperate to get it back.*"

I nodded, still looking over the map.

Balder went on. "*I traveled east, hiding from his army, until I eventually left the reach of where his troops were searching the area.*" He rolled the map back together, and tucked the scroll away into his robe. "*Then, it was just a matter of avoiding the normal undead at night, and taking the long way home.*"

"*Master,*" Kumara said. "*We should move the iron blocks. The skeletons will return any moment now, I'm sure, and will surely search your chest...*"

"*The Minecraftians have many chests in their home here*," I said in their minds. "*We can store them there*."

Balder looked back and forth between both of us in thought, then said, "*Yes, that's probably a good idea*." He looked at his apprentice. "*Make it so, Kumara*."

The apprentice nodded, and disappeared into the small dwelling. Returning with the blocks, he put them in the central chest of the Minecraftian house—the same chest where I had deposited all of the food before.

Later in the afternoon, WolfBroJake and Xenocide99 returned from mining. It appeared that they didn't make much progress.

But as I told them about the master blacksmith returning, and why there were now *one hundred and sixty-four* iron blocks in their chest, Balder himself suddenly *burst* into the house, eyes wide with alarm!

"*What is it, Balder?*" I asked in his mind.

"*They're here!*" he thought.

The Minecraftians would have just heard "Hurr!!"

"*Skeletons?*" I asked, rising to my feet.

"*Yes,*" he said. "*A dozen of them. Acting just like before.*"

He closed the door to the Minecraftians' home after him, and ducked down inside, watching from the window. The master smith must have been afraid of being seen, having escaped his prison at the castle. I looked down at Xenocide99 and WolfBroJake, who had no idea what was going on.

"*A squad of skeleton archers has arrived,*" I said into their minds. "*We must hide, like before.*"

"Hide?" WolfBroJake asked. "Why not *kill* them this time?! I'm tired of hiding..."

"*Are you ready to face the army?*" I asked. "*You are still under-armored. If we fight them now, if they figure out that we're here, the Skeleton King will come after the beacon and send his whole—*"

I stopped.

The Minecraftians and the blacksmith all watched me.

I heard the clattering of the skeleton's bones as they marched in single file down the cobblestone street toward the blacksmith's home...

Thinking back to the battle, I suddenly recalled the Skeleton King's orders to Balder before I stole the artifact...

"*Prisoner!*" the abomination had bellowed. "*Install the last block! Start the new power!*"

"What?!" Xenocide99 cried. "What is it??"

I looked down at the master blacksmith.

"*Balder, you know how to work the beacon, don't you??*"

"*Yes,*" he said. "*I do...*"

"*Yes! That's it!*" I exclaimed in all of their minds. "*Attack, Minecraftians! Kill them! Kill them all ... but one! Leave one alive!*"

The Minecraftians looked at each other, confused by the change in my directions, but then smiled, and stood, drawing their swords.

"Now *that's* what I like to hear!" WolfBroJake exclaimed.

"You've *got* something, don't you, ninja?" Xenocide99 said. "You've got a plan!"

"Yes, Xenocide99. Just make sure to leave one of them alive. Let's go!"

With that, we attacked, the Minecraftians springing from the door of the house and charging into battle.

Zip.

I teleported through the empty doorway, and saw, from the street, that the column of undead archers was *just now* approaching the Minecraftians' house. In another moment, and we would have seen them marching by through the windows, on their way to the blacksmith building.

The squad of skeletons stopped, surprised, and raised their bows, their eyes glowing red from empty, black sockets.

"Rraaaarrrr!"   WolfBroJake   shouted, charging into the lead skeleton with his shield held in front of him like a battering ram!

The warrior *crashed* into the archer at the front of the line, ruining the skeleton's shot and knocking the creature back into the next two undead behind it. His sword came down, and worked quickly.

Xenocide99, with his sword drawn but without a shield, ran in the other direction, darting around the house and down the alley.

Attacking the rear, I thought. He'll be coming up behind them.

Zip.

I warped into the middle of the column, and exploded into action, my fists and feet connecting with helmeted skulls and armored rib cages. Bones shattered and showered to the ground around me before the archers closest to me had a chance to react.

A nearby archer managed to recover from the ambush, and aimed his bow at me. Drew the arrow back...

Zip.

With a short warp, I moved just a little ways down the line of undead. It was a tight place to fight, after all.

Using a rapid combination of palm strikes, I shattered the nearest skeleton, then flipped a quick kick up to another. My foot caught the archer's helmet, and knocked it off of its head. The late afternoon sunlight set the skeleton on fire.

Reaching out with my *Chi*, I tried to *feel* the archers around me, to stay focused on any arrows coming at me from behind...

Dropping low, I swept the legs of another skeleton, knocking it to the ground, then delivered an *axe kick* to its chest, smashing it into bones!

Thunk.

It was a good thing that I dropped low for that *leg sweep*, because an arrow *just* missed me, and struck the cobblestone wall of the house across the street.

Don't try, I told myself. *Do*. I couldn't focus on arrows coming at me from all around—I had to let my *Chi* pick up on unseen danger *for* me...

Taking a quick glance around, I saw that the dozen skeletons were mostly decimated. WolfBroJake and Xenocide99 were cutting through them, heading to the center, and I was surrounded by several destroyed archers myself.

Two skeletons remained.

The first raised its bow at me. Like lightning, I snapped my hand out and knocked the bow out of its grip. The weapon went clattering off down the cobblestone walkway.

The second skeleton watched its comrade's bow fall, then looked back up at me, just in time to see my strikes coming at it with blinding speed— two palm strikes to knock it off balance, then I spun and delivered a powerful kick into its armored chest. The archer flew backward into the house on the other side of the street, and shattered into bones and dust...

All alone, the last undead archer, disarmed, turned and fled.

We let it run away.

It moved through the streets as fast as its clumsy bone legs would allow, turning down corner after corner, sending the villagers running away from it at every turn, until the archer finally broke out into the open, and escaped to the darkness of the forest...

"*Back to the Skeleton King*," I said into the Minecraftians' minds.

Xenocide99 put his sword away. "That was *awesome!*" he cried, grinning.

"I hope you have a good plan," WolfBroJake said. "We won't have long..."

Zip.

Teleporting back into the Minecraftians' home, I waited until Balder and the Minecraftians were with me. The master blacksmith sent for his apprentice, so we waited for Kumara as well.

Then I told them my plan.

Night 16 – Overworld

Zip.

I warped through the forest heading to the north...

Zip.

There wasn't much time. And with the time it would take to get *back* to the village *with her*, I'd have to get back to the cave as quickly as I could.

Assuming I could convince her to come with me...

Zip.

Back in the village, the Minecraftian males would be working through the night to construct a *wall*, then mining for iron and more cobblestone when they ran out of materials.

Even though Xenocide99 and WolfBroJake were having a hard time finding iron ore in the hills near the village, and Kumara was *also* having difficulty finding iron with his villager workers, no one ever counted on Balder's knowledge of the best places to mine near town.

The old master blacksmith had many secrets up his sleeves, including the locations of rich veins of ore that, up until now, he had kept to himself...

Now that the freedom of Overworld in this area, as well as the village and its people, were at risk, he happily shared the information.

Balder's apprentice would be deep in the mines by now, along with his helpers, to gather as much iron ore as they could before the Skeleton King arrived with his army.

Zip.

But what if the abomination didn't come? I thought.

He would come...

Balder was sure of it, and so was I.

The Skeleton King had apparently been busy these last few days scouring the region for the

Enderman that dared to attack him and steal his beacon.

He wanted *me*.

And that skeleton archer that escaped from our ambush had gotten a very good look at me...

The Skeleton King would come.

Zip.

That meant that we would have, at the very least, enough time to prepare for the attack as the time it took for the undead archer to return to the castle, tell the Skeleton King about us, and however long it would take for the monster to mobilize and march some *or all* of his army to the village.

The skeleton survivor was undead, so it would walk without stopping, without resting, until it returned to its master. It would travel *all night* back to the castle. And, once the Skeleton King got going, his army would march tirelessly to the north just the same.

So I had to move quickly as well.

At the very *soonest*, the army would arrive tomorrow night...

Zip.

I warped to the north as effectively as I could, resting and meditating to restore my *Chi* only when I needed to. After all—I wouldn't be able to teleport *back* to the village in the same way if LuckyMist returned with me. We would have to walk. I would get the rest I needed then...

Zip.

In time, over the course of the night, I warped through the huge forest, emerged into the long valley, and eventually, saw the imposing stone mountain up ahead.

Teleporting around the mountain through the forest on its east side, I arrived once again facing the cobblestone walls and two wooden doors, with the desert and *Nexus 426* at my back.

The square moon hung part-way down the sky.

It would be morning in a few hours, but I arrived here sooner than I expected!

Both doors were closed.

Approaching the window of the little cave home, I peered into the darkness inside. Reaching out with my tired *Chi*, I listened for LuckyMist's distinct energy.

There she was, sleeping in bed, a red blanket pulled over her small Minecraftian form.

I looked down at the door.

How does this darn thing open? I thought.

Feeling around the edges of the wooden door with my long, slender fingers, I tried again to see if I could find the secret of opening the contraption—I pushed at its edges, pried at its corners. I tapped areas of it with a dark fingertip, to see if it was anything like our *End Rod technology*, or operated at all like the controls of an *End Ship*...

Crossing my arms, I glared at the door.

I closed my eyes, and reached out to LuckyMist's mind, but it was shrouded in a sea of sleep...

"*LuckyMist*," I said into her mind.

I waited. Nothing.

"*LuckyMist*," I repeated. "*Awaken, Minecraftian! We need your help!*"

The veil of energy in her mind was thick and difficult to pierce. Of course it was—she was sleeping. I'd never tried to communicate with a being before when they were *sleeping*. Endermen don't sleep, so I didn't really understand how to interpret the strange energy I was picking up off of her. It was as if she was, quite simply, *turned off*. And yet, beneath the surface of this thick, deadened cloud, I could barely sense a *torrent* of energy. There was a lot going on in there, under the murky surface of LuckyMist's mind...

Looking back down to the door, I tried to remember all of the times I saw the Minecraftians and villagers use the darned things...

Of course, I thought.

My eyes darted to the carved wooden contraption that stuck out from the surface near the opening edge. I don't know why I didn't think about it before—maybe because it was so low.

But it wasn't low for the Minecraftians at all—there was a wooden *handle* of some kind, right about at *waist level*.

Reaching out, I touched it.

It jiggled, but the door didn't open.

I pulled on it, but it stayed in place.

Moving it from side-to-side, it jiggled in place again, but held firm. Twisting it, I—

Click.

The door opened...

I did it! I thought. *I figured out Minecraftian doors!*

Zip.

Warping in through the opening, I stood in the middle of the main room. Below me on one side, LuckyMist slept soundly in her bed.

The last time I stood in this *very place*, in the darkness of night, I was about to *kill* all three of the Minecraftians...

Looking around, I could see that the female had built the place back up again—there was a full complement of Minecraftian tools and gear. A crafting table, some furnaces, wooden storage containers...

Bending, I laid a hand on LuckyMist's shoulder, and gave her a gentle shake.

Her eyes popped open.

LuckyMist saw me standing over her, and sprang to her hands and feet, scrambling backwards away from me on the bed, gasping and moving her mouth as if screaming. Only a sound of quiet surprise emerged.

"What?! What's going on—who??"

I straightened, and stood back, to allow her to recover.

What happens to a creature that sleeps when the sleep is interrupted? I wondered.

"Ohmygod ... *Elias??* Elias? What are you doing here?" she stammered.

"*Greetings, LuckyMist,*" I said into her mind. The cloud of energy-deadening sleep was gone. "*I apologize for interrupting you in sleep...*"

LuckyMist stood on the stone floor, looked over and saw that the door was open, and walked over to the front of the room. She closed the door, and shook her head, as if trying to clear her *Chi.*

"Hi, no ... it's okay ... Elias ... what are you doing here? What do you want?"

"*The battle with the Skeleton King draws nigh,*" I responded. "*We need your help...*"

She shook her head again, and put her hands to her temples, closing her eyes and thinking to herself.

315

"No, Elias," she said quietly. "I told you, I'm *not* going to fight anymore. I'm sorry, but I'm not going to change my mind..."

I suddenly realized that if I just said everything I said before, again, that I would leave this place *without her* once again.

Something had to be different. She wouldn't change her mind, unless I was *open* with her.

"*I'm sorry, LuckyMist*," I said into her mind. "*I am truly sorry for leading you into danger ... carelessly.*"

She looked up.

"*I realize now, Minecraftian, that my mind was not in the right place. I let my ... ego ... get in the way of my skills, and my good sense, and...*"

This was hard to put into words. It was difficult to bear my true feelings to anyone other than my master...

"*When we joined forces, you Minecraftians and I, and visited the village, at that point I felt like*

316

I was the strongest I'd ever been, and I let my feelings cloud my judgment. I ... cared more about completing my mission and increasing my rank in the Order than I did about ... you three, and..."

"Oh, it's okay, Elias," she said. "You did very well there, you weren't careless with us—"

"But I was," I interrupted. *"I never considered your safety, until the moment of being in the battle when you three were in trouble. We went into the attack with a very simple plan. I should have given it more thought—should have considered a stronger strategy. I should have planned to preserve your safety. But I left you three to fight the entire army, toe-to-toe as WolfBroJake would say, and never considered that anything could go wrong. It was foolish. I played with your lives, and I'm sorry."*

My *Chi* suddenly felt a warm burst of energy from the little Minecraftian, and she approached, taking one of my hands.

"Thank you, Elias," she said. "But we're okay now. We always come *back*, remember?"

"*I was reckless,*" I said. "*And I will not be reckless with you again.*"

We stood quiet for a while.

"So, what's your plan?" she asked. "Just— out of curiosity…"

I told her. I related to her the return of the blacksmith and the iron cubes. The skeleton archers and the ambush. The Skeleton King's search for me and the beacon. WolfBroJake and Xenocide99 building the walls and mining iron from Balder's secret mines…

"*And we expect the Skeleton King to march on the village by tomorrow night at the earliest. If you were to … come and help … we would have to hurry there.*"

She thought on it.

"Okay," LuckyMist said. "Let's do it. I like your plan. Let me get some stuff. Can we wait until morning?"

"*No,*" I responded. "*We need to leave as soon as you are able. Time is of the essence. I'll*

318

protect you as we travel in the dark ... if that's okay with you, that is."

She nodded, then took some things from the chests in the main room, and disappeared down into her mine.

When LuckyMist returned, she was outfitted in a brand new set of iron armor.

"You've been busy," I said into her mind.

"I'm a good miner," she responded with a smile. "And I have some iron to bring with us, too."

After LuckyMist situated her gear, and broke down her bed to take with her, we departed to the south. There was still at least an hour before dawn, so we walked intently through the dark, the female Minecraftian peering around with a torch in her hand, and I, ready to divert any of the natural mobs in the area that would be inclined to attack...

At times, zombies and other creatures approached, and I was able to convince *some* of them to turn around and leave us alone with my *mind voice*.

Other times, an occasional mob couldn't be persuaded to hold off its attack, and I had to *smash* it into the ground.

We moved with speed, and tried to avoid resting. LuckyMist snacked on pieces of Minecraftian food here and there as we continued traveling to the south, waiting for the sun to rise...

Pssssst!!
Liking the story? Don't forget to join my Mailing List! I'll send you *free books* and stuff! (www.SkeletonSteve.com)

Day 17 – Overworld

By the time the moon sank below the horizon and the sun crept up in the east, we had made it to the other side of the long valley. As the sky brightened and the roaming undead caught on fire, we passed the place where WolfBroJake and Xenocide99 had killed the herd of cows when we last passed through here together.

Traveling intently through the morning, with LuckyMist trying to conserve energy by being quiet and determined, I tried to restore my *Chi* by relaxing my mind and pulling energy from the many pearl seed blocks of dirt hidden in the land around me.

At times, we chatted briefly about what happened after LuckyMist died.

I told her about my one-on-one battle with the Skeleton King, about how I narrowly managed to escape by carefully warping away with the little *Chi* I had left, and how I used the Minecraftians' cave next to *boot rock* to hide in until I could teleport back to The End.

She told me that the battle and the escape sounded *horrible*.

I told her about the training I did with my master back in the Temple after I had healed, and how I was getting help from Xenocide99 and WolfBroJake in exercising my *Chi Dodge*.

Eventually, we made it back to the village around noon.

The sun was high in the sky when we stepped out of the forest and into the grassy field, and I was surprised—and dismayed—to see a very impressive defensive wall of stone built around the village ... a wall that was still very *unfinished*.

Approaching on foot with LuckyMist, I inspected the layout of the new defenses. The Minecraftians still had a long way to go, but the beginnings of a wall completely encasing the village and its farm plots was in place—even though it was still short enough for me to step over in many places.

The cobblestone wall was simple, and extended around the village on all four sides, with one exception:

On the southern side of the village, the side closest to the castle from where the skeleton troops always arrived had an *extra layer*—an *extra* wall. On the south side, there was an *inner* wall, and an *outer* wall, with a large open space in between.

This walled-in open space—this *battlefield*—would be where I hoped to encourage the fight to take place. Once the Skeleton King breached the outer wall on the southern side, his forces would have to advance through the large open field before needing to break through the second *inner* wall to get to the actual village.

Zip.

It still needed a lot of work, but I could imagine the battle and see the forces moving, looking over the entire area from atop the village's watch tower. Well over a hundred skeletons could fit inside the walled field. And if I could get the battle to move *into* there, the village and its people would be protected during the fight.

WolfBroJake and Xenocide99 were gone. They must have run out of stone, and were in the mines.

Zip.

Down at the blacksmith building, I asked Kumara to direct LuckyMist to where the others were working. She would want to help down there, and could probably mine as fast as WolfBroJake and Xenocide99 put together...

Once she was gone to join the other Minecraftians, I searched for Balder.

I found the master blacksmith assembling an iron block pyramid inside the attic of the village church building.

"*Hello, master smith,*" I said into his mind. "*Is everything going according to plan?*"

He looked up from his work, startled that I was standing behind him suddenly.

"*Uh, yes, Enderman. And look!*" he thought, gesturing around at the large, open attic of the village's largest structure. "*This attic has plenty of room to hide the iron pyramid. When I'm finished here, we'll just have to remove the block in the roof directly above the beacon to let it shine into the sky…*"

"*Very good, Balder,*" I responded. "*The wall looks like it's taking longer than I thought.*"

He shook his head. "*Yes, it is. A wall of that size takes a lot of stone. Far more than the Minecraftians and our village had in stock. The two Minecraftians and the village workers are down in the mines right now collecting iron and more stone.*"

"*If we can't finish the wall before tonight, and the Skeleton King arrives then, the plan won't work if his forces overwhelm the village from another direction.*"

"*I understand, Ender,*" Balder said. "*We will work on the wall as quickly as we can. Once I'm done setting up the beacon, I'll help with the wall myself.*"

"*As will I,*" I responded, "*until I have to prepare for the battle.*"

For a while, I walked around the village, conserving my energy and trying to recharge my *Chi*. I would need it *all* for the battle. Even if I could master the *Chi Dodge*, I would still need my *Chi* to be strong enough to warp whenever I needed to evade the enemy...

Suddenly, I was surprised when the blue sky was *split open* by a brilliant beam of light, stabbing upwards as high as I could see ... from *inside* the church building!

The beacon was amazing!

The column of light pierced the blue of the sky with such intensity that—

And it wasn't *red!* It was white...

The beacon light was white!

Why? I thought. Why did it change colors now?

Was it just different because Balder was programming it for us differently than he programmed it for the Skeleton King? Or was it a simple matter of the darkness and light of our different *Chi?* The Skeleton King, even without the beacon, was fully enveloped by that strange, evil *red* energy. Maybe the beacon was *naturally* white, and was corrupted by the presence of the red energy of the abomination? Or corrupted by being aligned with the monster?

It didn't matter.

As long as the beacon worked for us, it could be any color it wanted...

Zip.

I appeared at the entrance of the church, and warped up into the attic just in time to see Balder standing before the blazing column of white light, its brilliance bathing the room and reflecting on the master blacksmith's face as he delivered an ingot of iron into the burning light.

The chunk of metal dissolved in its brilliance.

"Everything okay?" I asked in his mind.

327

The energy in the room was loud, but it was good. It did not sicken me like the red energy did back in the castle. The beacon was now a power that would *help* us.

"*Yes,*" Balder thought. "*I'm just programming it now…*"

"*But now that we have the beacon active and lit,*" I said, "*it can be seen for miles around in the sky. The Skeleton King may not even attack if he sees it. Does it have to shoot up into the sky like that?*"

"*I'm afraid so,*" he said. "*Or its powers will be useless to you.*"

"Can we hide it?"

"*If you do, the powers will be useless until you let it back into the sky again…*"

Zip.

Warping back down into the street, I looked around for a moment, then pulled up a block of dirt from a nearby yard.

Zip.

Up on the roof of the church, I approached the hole in the cobblestone structure that bled the brilliant, white light. The beacon's blaze erupted from the hole in the roof—constant, intense, and powerful...

Plop.

I plugged up the hole with a block of dirt.

Just like *that*, the column of light was gone, and the sky was normal again...

Making my way back to the attic, I saw Balder still working with beacon, standing atop the massive pyramid of metal cubes, somehow manipulating the artifact with his hands. The beacon was still active, even though the roof was plugged up, and shot a blazing column of light up to the ceiling, where it stopped and sizzled and spit motes of harmless white fire all around the rafters.

"Still working okay?" I asked.

"Yes, that'll do it," Balder said. *"Just don't forget to open it up again when the fighting starts!"*

Later, I met with the Minecraftians and the village workers who emerged from the mine.

The three Minecraftians seemed very happy to be reunited again, and I tried to help them as they busily worked on the wall, block by block, raising it little by little, all around the village as the sun sank lower and lower into the sky...

I tried to help. The cobblestone wasn't easy for me to work with. I've never had any trouble with *dirt*, of course. That's what we Ender do—walk the Overworld, checking the dirt blocks for ender pearl seeds. But the cobblestone was slow to move and place. And whenever I made a mistake and set a block down in the wrong spot, I had to wait for a Minecraftian to come and cut it loose for me again.

The Minecraftians, on the other hand, were in their *element*.

Placing and organizing and moving blocks for them was like *child's play*. They laid down cobblestone like an artist moving a paintbrush—and whenever they needed anything undone, they could remove the cobblestone just as quickly with their tools.

But we were running out of time...

As the sky started to change color and the sun began to set, everyone in the village that was *able* was helping to complete the wall.

We weren't going to make it...

There were still open areas and incomplete sections.

At lease the strategic front area would be complete.

As the sun went down and the sky turned silver, then dark blue, I teleported to the roof of the Minecraftians' home to meditate and recharge my *Chi*.

The Minecraftians were still trying to finish the wall when the villagers all fled to their little houses, slamming their doors behind them.

Night 17 – Overworld

The first hour of the night was uneventful, and the Minecraftians finally managed to *finish* the wall!

Meditating on the roof, my pearl felt warm as my *Chi* rolled over me in waves, picking up on the *Chi* of the seed blocks all around me. I felt strong. My *Chi* was healthy and ready.

I heard Xenocide99 munching on something as the three of them ran back to the house.

"Now let's make that *armor*," WolfBroJake said. "It'll be good to have real armor again."

"Yeah, we should have enough for you guys," LuckyMist said.

Xenocide99 spoke in between bites. "We got almost got enough for a whole suit of armor today in the mine! If you have enough for a breastplate and some greaves, we should be good, honey!"

Standing, I took a few steps, and dropped down silently onto the cobblestone street below. As the Minecraftians opened the door and poured inside the house, I followed.

Zip.

"Oh!" LuckyMist exclaimed. "Hi, Elias!"

"Hey, man," WolfBroJake said. "How's the beacon?"

I walked over to an open area of the room, and sat down, crossing my legs under me. Counting the beds, I noticed that LuckyMist had added her 'spawn point' to the others' once again.

"The beacon is ready," I said into their minds. *"I will unleash its power when the battle begins."*

"What'll it do?" Xenocide99 asked. "Make us *super-fast* and stuff like the skeletons?"

"I don't know," I responded. *"Balder programmed it, and said he controlled its power to give us the greatest advantage against the army."*

334

"I wonder what a villager blacksmith thinks *that* would be...?" WolfBroJake said.

The three of them began eating.

"The wall is finished?" I asked.

"It is," LuckyMist responded. "We even doubled up the normal outer walls. Why did you want *two* doors on the southern-most outer wall? *One door* would work better for defense. If those double-doors are broken, it'll be easier for the army to get in!"

"I think that's the idea," WolfBroJake said.

I nodded.

After dinner, the two males began working their iron into pieces of armor at the crafting table.

"Guys, I also brought something else," LuckyMist said. "Something for *all* of us." She looked at me. "Well—all three *Minecraftians*, anyway. I don't think this would be very useful to you, Elias..."

She opened her pack.

"What is it?" Xenocide99 said.

LuckyMist pulled six glittering blue stones from her inventory.

"*Diamonds?*" WolfBroJake asked.

"Yeah," she said. "I found them yesterday. *Finally*." She laughed. "I was saving them, but being as we're here now, and going into a big fight again, I figured we may as well use them to make *swords*..."

The males grinned and cheered, and the three Minecraftians carefully used the diamonds and other resources to craft three eloquent and stout weapons. The resulting blades looked like chipped stone—like chipped *glass*—and glimmered dangerously in the torchlight.

"Awesome..." WolfBroJake said, grinning ear to ear, testing the balance of his new weapon.

I suddenly remembered the day I stepped onto the Temple bridge, returning from my *Seed Stride* to be given this mission by my master. Sitting on the bridge, meditating to harness his *Chi* to heal his nasty wounds, was a middle ninja—a skilled adult of full rank—who had lost a battle against two Minecraftians armed with these...

Diamond swords.

The destructive technology my friends now held in their hands made me wary, but if they were on *my* side, it couldn't be that bad...

The Minecraftians stayed awake, ready, and we were expecting to hear the clattering of bones and the approach of the Skeleton King's army at any moment.

"Maybe they're not coming," Xenocide99 said.

For a while, I started to think that he may be right...

But then they *did* come.

The sound of the bones clunking around in the distance was faint, but my *Chi* alerted me to the army's presence long before the Minecraftians noticed.

"*They're here,*" I said into their minds. "*Let's go!*"

The Minecraftians stopped talking, straining to listen. Their eyes went wide, and they jumped to their feet, grabbing their new shields.

Zip.

Warping out the door, I led them through the village, through the inner wall, across the battlefield, and to the outer wall where we would eventually engage the army.

Now, standing together inside the double-doors of the south outer wall, I could tell that the three warriors heard the hundreds of bones *clunking* as the undead army emerged from the forest.

"*Remember the plan,*" I said into their minds. "*We'll stand on the wall, and you three attack with your bows until they break through the doors. Then, fall back, and we'll attack them with the aid of the beacon once they're inside. And when you shoot at them, keep in mind that perhaps a hundred archers might shoot back at you...*"

"Got it," WolfBroJake said. The others nodded.

Zip.

Warping up on the wall, I saw the Minecraftians running up the cobblestone stairs to join me.

Yes, I thought. *The army.*

He must have brought his *entire* army.

Looking out into the darkness on the other side of the outer wall, into the shadows of the forest to the south of the grassy plain, I saw scores of red, glowing eyes looking back at me. And in the middle of them, the hulking figure of the Skeleton King...

The abomination stood tall and strong, his bones massive and thick, the armor on his shoulders and giant black bow on his right arm gleaming in the moonlight.

His eyes blazed red, and *flared* when they met mine...

"Enderman!" the Skeleton King yelled across the space with a booming voice.

Reaching out with my *Chi*, I felt the familiar sickening red energy that poured out from his mind, and responded.

"*Hello, Skeleton King,*" I said into his head. "*Have you been looking for me?*"

"Still the arrogant punk, huh, young one?" he bellowed. "Need me to teach you a lesson *again?*"

"*I have indeed learned from you, monster,*" I responded.

"This time, I'll pound you into Ender *paste*, thief! You won't get away this time!"

"*Here for your beacon, I presume?*"

"It's *mine*, Enderman! Give it to me now, so that I don't break it when I crush you again..."

"*I rather like it,*" I responded. "*I think I'd like to keep it.*"

The Skeleton King's eyes flared, casting a red glow over the scores of armored skeleton archers surrounding him. With great speed, he

340

raised his bow arm, and fired one of his long, black arrows my way.

Easy.

Zip.

I warped a few feet to the side, and let the spear-like arrow sail past me into the night.

"*So that's it for talking?*" I asked into his mind.

The monster's eyes flared in anger again, and he pointed at me with a thick, bony finger.

"*Attack!*" he roared. "Kill them all! The Enderman, the Minecraftians, the villagers—every living thing inside those walls!!"

With that, the skeleton army moved as a coordinated unit, stepping forward together, raising their bows in unison, moving as a great square of undead troops, straight for the southern wall.

In the corner of my vision, I could see the Minecraftians lobbing long shots at them with their own bows. Three arrows flew through the air. One of them—probably Xenocide99's—struck a skeleton in the front line directly in the chest. It staggered, but continued its approach.

The sound of the undead marching in lock-step was loud and haunting.

Clunk clunk clunk clunk clunk clunk...

It reminded me of the sounds they made when I faced down the Skeleton King before.

The Minecraftians fired again, launching their arrows in an arc, high into the sky.

Another skeleton staggered, wounded, and a second fell to pieces, destroyed.

And then they were in range.

As a group, the skeleton archers stopped, aimed high, and fired a hundred or so bows at our position. A volley of arrows flew through the air, almost impossible to see in the dark.

"Whoa!!" WolfBroJake cried as the three of them ducked behind our crude battlements, raising their shields against the assault. Arrows rained down upon us.

This wouldn't do...

Zip.

Warping across the grassy field outside the outer wall, over the battery of archers, past the Skeleton King, I appeared suddenly behind the abomination, leaving a trail of glowing motes of purple light in my *warp path*. The Skeleton King, shocked, followed the purple lights with his eyes, turning, until he was suddenly facing me.

Crunch.

"Rraaarrr!"

The monster cried out in pain as I struck him in the face with a blindingly fast *palm strike*, then warped away again, instantly back to the wall...

Zip.

Appearing back in my original position, I looked at the surprised faces of the Minecraftians who had just witnessed my extremely bold move. Their shields already showed several arrows stuck in the wood from the army's first attack.

Ego, they must have thought. *Reckless*.

"*Don't worry*," I said into their minds. "*I won't do that again…*"

The Skeleton King roared in a fury from the field below, and his army of archers parted down the middle as he charged, lumbering and heavy, toward the double-doors below me.

Returning fire, the Minecraftians harassed the vastly superior number of archers below them, then ducked out of the way again as arrows sailed around us.

Boom!

The Skeleton King slammed his heavy body into the doors.

"Ghasts!" he bellowed from below. "*Attack!!*"

Boom!

The doors shuttered again.

"Ghasts??" WolfBroJake asked, then looked up to the sky.

344

As if on cue, I heard a chilling sound come from the night sky—that of a mix between a wounded animal and a crying child. Something called out from the darkness, and with my vision—unhindered by the night—I saw the creatures descend from high above...

Boom!

The Skeleton King pounded on the doors again. The wood splintered. The archers fired again, and we took cover.

Three ... no ... *four* large, white creatures of *nightmare* descended from the sky...

How did I not notice them before??

They were almost as big as the smallest villager houses—monstrous creatures. Pale and bloated, with puffy eyes sealed closed with ichor that also ran down their sunken faces, the floating *ghasts* moved slowly through the air and trailed long, white tentacles behind them.

Boom!

With a final crash, I heard the doors sunder beneath me in the wall, and I saw the skeleton army surge forward through the hole, all following their king as he charged into the field—our 'battlefield'—with thundering footsteps.

A hideous other-worldly cry sounded above, I looked up just in time to see one of the ghasts open its stuck eyes—red swollen things—and its withered mouth launch a fireball down at me from above. The speedy ball of flame flew straight at me, and I was reminded of my training with Master Ee'char...

Zip.

Teleporting to another area of the southern wall, I extended my *Chi,* like I had been practicing, so that I would hopefully *sense* any arrows flying my way, and use the *Chi Dodge* to evade them.

The fireball hit where I was standing before my teleport, exploding with a loud blast, shaking the cobblestone and sending chunks of rock and mortar showering down to the ground.

"Holy cow!!" Xenocide99 cried. He put his back to the nearest battlement, and fired his bow at the nearest floating monstrosity.

Looking down, I saw the Skeleton King on the battlefield, in between the outer and inner walls just where I wanted him, just in time to see him taking aim at me with his massive bow...

Zip.

Warping out of the way, the big, black arrow flew through the air and speared itself into the battlement behind where I had been standing.

The undead archers where streaming into the battlefield through the broken double-doors...

Despite the *ghasts*, everything was going according to plan!

"*Okay!*" I said into the Minecraftians' heads. "*Stay away from the Skeleton King! Protect yourselves! I'm going to open up the beacon!*"

"Got it!" yelled WolfBroJake.

Just then, another ghast made its creepy scream from above, and I heard another fireball launch through the air. LuckyMist looked up just in time to see the ball of fire bolting straight at *her*.

"Look out!" Xenocide99 yelled, launching another arrow at the ghasts. I didn't notice if he'd hit one yet or not.

Unable to get out of the way quickly enough, LuckyMist raised her shield just as the fireball *crashed* into the wall next to her, and I watched in shock as she fell off the other side, plummeting down into the mass of skeleton archers trying to swarm into the opening.

She screamed.

She was *outside* the outer wall...

"*I'll get her—hold out!*" I yelled into their minds.

WolfBroJake and Xenocide99 looked shocked and unsure, but moved to be closer together.

Zip.

I warped to the other side of the wall, as close as I could manage to where I thought LuckyMist fell.

It wasn't a long fall—the wall wasn't very high—but she had fallen right into the midst of the undead army. I was pleased to see that she was already on her feet, holding her shield up, trying to ward off the arrows of the nearest skeletons.

Zip.

Appearing next to her, I let loose a flurry of kicks and palm strikes, knocking all of the closest archers backwards or shattering them into broken bones.

"*Run!*" I said into her mind. "*Go back around the corner!*"

This was bad...

I should have unleashed the power of the beacon by now. Instead, we were separated. WolfBroJake and Xenocide99 were on their own, dealing with the Skeleton King, countless archers, *and* four of those *ghast* creatures. And LuckyMist and I were on the other side of the wall!

It was a good thing that the skeleton archers were so focused on swarming into the hole left by the smashed double-doors.

After carefully backing away with her shield, LuckyMist was able to get away into the night, turning around the corner of the west wall. I followed, destroying a handful of undead archers along the way. Two more ghast fireballs flew down from above and exploded on the walls. The cobblestone shuddered next to us, sending pebbles and dust falling onto our heads.

"Can you get over the wall?" I asked LuckyMist.

"Yes!!" she cried. "I have dirt!"

Stashing the bow she was still holding, LuckyMist pulled out blocks of dirt, and built herself up the wall with a small dirt tower, letting her reach the top quickly.

Those *Minecraftians* and their blocks...

Zip.

Teleporting back up to the wall, I surveyed the situation.

The ghasts were surrounding us. Two of them had descended lower, and the other two were hanging pretty high up in the sky. Launching fireballs with a casual ease, the Nether monsters were unhurried and disorganized, but deadly.

The Skeleton King was still down on the battlefield inside the walls, now surrounded by the majority of his army, and they all moved together taking shots at WolfBroJake and Xenocide99, who scrambled around on the wall, dodging constantly, taking cover behind their shields and blocks of battlements. From time to time, the Minecraftian males returned fire, sending back occasional potshots.

WolfBroJake and Xenocide99 were already wounded, their armor blackened from the ghasts' explosions and bristling with arrows.

At least they hadn't been hit by the Skeleton King!

Yet.

I had to get to that beacon!!

"*LuckyMist, do what you can! Help the others—protect yourselves! I have to unleash the beacon!*"

I thought, in that moment, that I should have arranged for Balder to wait in the church to remove the dirt block himself. If there was one thing I was learning consistently from all of these battles, it was that things never went as they were planned!

When I fought the Minecraftians before, I didn't count on them reappearing in their beds!

When I fought the Skeleton King the *last* time, I didn't count on him still being a very capable fighter after I disabled the 'artifact'—the beacon that was definitely *not* the source of his power!

And this time, I didn't count on having to rescue LuckyMist from the wrong side of the wall, and being *delayed* on releasing the beacon, the cornerstone of our strategy! I also didn't anticipate the Skeleton King having more than just archers on his side.

Even with much more careful planning, I always had ideas in the moment of truth of ways that I could have prepared better. And things always went wrong that we couldn't have ever prepared for...

Thunk.

I grimaced as an arrow struck me in the side. Too late. Not paying attention. Not *feeling*...

Zip.

Far away from the battle, on the roof of the church, I could see the ghasts drifting through the sky above the battle like leaves floating on a pond. Their fireballs streaked across the sky, and in the flash of the explosions, I saw that it was three Minecraftians against a *whole army*...

Reaching down, I sank my fingers into the dirt block...

Pop.

The instant the dirt block was pulled from the cobblestone roof, I was dazzled by the blinding *white light* shooting straight up into the sky! The brilliant column burned with cold white fire, stabbing up and up, and I could feel its power *pour* into me...

My body suddenly felt *amazing* ... so alive ... so *strong!* All of my nerves were on fire, and I wanted nothing more than to lay into the entire horde of undead troops, to *crush* them under my fists and kicks—to grind them into dust...

Zip.

I appeared on the battlefield, a massive group of archers around me.

Up on the wall, I could see the Minecraftians huddled together, staring at the brilliant column of white light behind me as it pierced the sky from the church roof. The bright light reflected in their eyes and shone on their armor.

We would be okay, I thought.

I cut into the undead like a wildfire...

Extending my *Chi*, I tried to feel the energy—the *Chi*—of the world around me, and I could *almost* sense all of the little things. It was like I was the center of a pool of water, and everything moving around me alerted me with little *ripples*.

I could *feel*.

And the beacon made me feel *strong*. Unstoppable.

Undead archers shattered before me.

I am a strong, fierce martial artist.

But now, under the effect of the beacon, I was a *juggernaut*...

The Minecraftians can feel it too! I thought, looking up to the wall as my hands and feet did their deadly dance around me.

WolfBroJake and LuckyMist pulled their diamond swords and charged together down the stairs, pushing the tide of undead back with their shields and cutting through them like their bones were made of sticks! Xenocide99 stood tall and took confident shots at the ghasts with his bow, sidestepping the fireballs without fear.

They weren't looking so *wounded* anymore...

Thunk.

An arrow pierced my arm.

Still not quite right, I thought. My *Chi Dodge* was imperfect.

Amidst the chaos of the battle, I heard a new cry from one of the ghasts, and I looked up to see one of them struck by Xenocide99's arrow. The monster let out a strange whine as it seems to ... *deflate* ... and then disappear.

"Got one!!" Xenocide99 yelled over the battle.

Arrows flew at me.

Zip zip zip.

I dodged, but did it consciously.

I had to *let go*...

The key to the *Chi Dodge* was to trust in my *Chi*...

Thunk.

Another arrow struck me, this time in the chest.

Under the effects of the beacon, I hardly felt the pain.

Zip.

Up until now, I was slaughtering all of the skeleton archers that were within my reach. I wasn't even paying attention anymore. My body and my martial skills did the work, and bones smashed and scattered under my hands and feet. Instead, I was thinking about my *Chi* and the *Chi Dodge*.

But now, I warped away as my swath of death and destruction made its way to the Skeleton King, and the massive monster took a swing at me with a heavy, bony arm.

Not yet, I thought.

On the other side of the army, WolfBroJake and LuckyMist were doing *just fine* cutting through the undead around them. They bristled with arrows, and looked like they had taken plenty of hits through their shields and armor, but didn't look like they were having any trouble.

Their diamond swords carved paths through the archers, dropping the skeletons and splitting their bones into pieces and shards wherever they passed.

I suddenly remembered the *last* battle, back at the castle, where I saw the skeletons' bones *mending*.

Ah ha! I thought.

Pausing, I pulled the arrow out of my chest, tossing it to the ground.

Zip.

My *Chi Dodge* worked that time, and moved me out of the way of an arrow coming at me unnoticed...

Looking down at my black skin, the black ichor of Ender blood seeping from the wound, I saw my dark flesh and skin ooze together and become whole again...

Regeneration.

I smiled.

Looking up, I saw the Skeleton King aiming at me with his huge bow.

Zip.

The black arrow launched through the air where I was standing, spearing into a skeleton archer instead. It shattered and fell.

We could *still* be killed—I killed plenty of skeletons who were regenerating, when they took enough damage...

Boom!

A ghast explosion sounded near me, and I felt tiny shards of rock and debris shower all around.

One of the floating things above let out another death cry, whining and deflating as Xenocide99 scored another good hit.

"Two down!" the Minecraftian archer shouted.

Thunk.

Another arrow struck me in the back.

Zip.

My *Chi Dodge* moved me out of the way of another.

I reached around and pulled the arrow from my back, then pulled the other one out of my arm that I'd been ignoring. With my *Chi*, I could feel a sort of *field* of energy around me. My pearl felt my surroundings like scattered noise of *pops* and *sparks* as arrows whistled through the air.

Taking a deep breath, I tried to *still my mind...*

"Your head and your body are still not one," Master Ee'char's voice reminded me.

But I'm trying, I thought.

I remembered his words again:

"*We must not learn to try harder. The key is to learn how not to try at all...*"

Closing my eyes, I listened to the energy field around me.

The noise of my *Chi* picking up the arrows and other small movements around me became louder...

And I let go...

I am the warping wind...

Letting my eyes crack open calmly, I found myself moving like lightning, crushing skulls, shattering ribcages with every movement.

Zip.

Something came at me—I didn't even notice. But I warped out of the way.

I moved like black death, my fists battering rams, my feet like *TNT*.

The beacon made me strong and nigh-unstoppable. So I destroyed everything undead within my reach.

Another ghost died above. I vaguely heard Xenocide99's cheer.

And when the fourth and last floating Nether creature was killed by Xenocide99's bow, I looked around, and found myself standing among *heaps* of shattered bones with WolfBroJake and LuckyMist. Xenocide99 was running down the stairs to join us. The Minecraftians appeared healthy, even though their armor was heavily damaged and many arrows protruded from their bodies.

We faced the Skeleton King across the battlefield—his army now reduced to twenty or so archers huddling around their leader...

"You *dare* use my own beacon against me, Enderman?!" the abomination bellowed.

The Skeleton King's eyes blazed red, and he fired his wicked, black bow at me.

Zip.

362

The black arrow flew past.

Zip.

With a *still mind*, I was suddenly standing behind him, shattering the undead archers that stood in my way.

The Skeleton King turned to face me, and the Minecraftians charged, laying into the skeleton archers that remained. The white light of the beacon gleamed in their dented armor…

"Are you ready for more, Enderma—"

The Skeleton King started to mock me with his booming voice, but I interrupted him with a powerful strike to the face. I felt his massive jawbone *crunch* under my palm.

With a little alarm in his undead face, the abomination raised his thick, bony arms to defend himself.

Using the great *strength boost* from the beacon, I batted one of his arms aside, and sent several speedy and strong punches into his body, splintering his mighty ribs with each hit.

The monster used his other arm to try and punch me, but I deflected the attack, redirected him into an arm-bar, then let out a mighty *kiai* roar and *broke* his massive elbow with a forceful blow!

The Skeleton King cried out in pain, his deep voice booming across the battlefield.

Zip.

My *Chi Dodge* moved me out of the way as the abomination's ribcage sprang open, trying to catch me in its *crushing trap* like he did to me in the last battle. The bizarre ribcage trap yawned open in the night, splitting up the middle like a sideways-clamshell, reaching out to crush me in its bony jaws...

But I wasn't there.

The ribcage snapped shut.

Standing a little off to his side, I let loose a roundhouse kick into the Skeleton King's hips, connecting with a satisfying *crunch*, and throwing the monster down and away from me.

The battlefield shook under my feet when the abomination fell to the ground.

Advancing to finish him off while he was down, I towered over the Skeleton King's huge form for a moment, before he lifted his bow with his good arm and aimed it at my head.

I didn't need the *Chi Dodge* for that...

Swaying slightly to the side, I dodged the shot easily, then darted in and pummeled the monster's massive skull face again and again...

The Skeleton King struggled to stand, and I relented my attack for just a moment as I looked into his red, flaring eyes.

Fear.

The monster's face looked battered and broken, and his eyes were losing their vigor.

He looked afraid...

Then he raised his bow to my head again.

Striking like lightning, I tried to swat the bow out of my way before he fired, but with the great strength given to me by the beacon, there was a splitting *crack*, and I knocked the bow off of his arm!

The huge, black bow flew through the night air, and landed in the field.

My *Chi* suddenly surged, and I felt that something big had changed...

There was a sudden *shift* in energy.

A big one...

I noticed that the Minecraftians were all done with the skeleton archers now, and were standing together, watching me fight the Skeleton King. We were surrounded by a field of bones.

The *red energy* that surrounded the Skeleton King was ... changing. It was gone!

Not gone entirely—just *moved* ... somewhere else.

Pausing my attack, standing over the broken Skeleton King, who feebly held his broken arm above him to defend himself, I realized that

366

the red energy surrounding his *Chi* was … dissipating…

Reaching out with my *Chi*, I could still feel it. My eyes and my *Chi* scanned my surroundings until they centered in on…

The bow.

It was *the bow*.

Looking back at the Skeleton King now below me, he suddenly seemed far less menacing. In fact, was he *smaller?*

Yes—smaller!

And smaller yet! The Skeleton King was shrinking before my very eyes, his bones becoming thinner, his skull and jaw becoming less … savage…

The shoulder armor he wore was suddenly far too big, and slipped off of his very *normal-sized* arms, falling to the ground with a *clang*. The huge, abomination ribcage that could open like the mouth of the Nether and swallow creatures whole … was now a *normal* ribcage, like all of the others I've shattered in a single blow. Holding a thin, broken arm above him, the Skeleton King was now small and frail below me...

So like a *normal* skeleton...

The abomination's face twisted in expressions of pain and fear—confusion and shock.

The monster had shrunken down to become a normal skeleton archer, like his minions, in every way!

Except for the eyes.

The skeleton's *eyes*, behind its looks of confusion and fear, still had those small, red pin pricks of light, darting around frantically in empty, black eye sockets...

I stood, and the terrified, wounded Skeleton King collapsed, curling up on the ground.

The Minecraftians approached, looking over the transformed monster in curiosity.

"What—?" WolfBroJake said.

"What happened??" Xenocide99 asked.

"The Skeleton King turned into a normal skeleton!" LuckyMist exclaimed.

"Well what are we waiting for?!" WolfBroJake said, raising his sword.

The skeleton on the ground gasped and hid his face.

"*No*," I said into their minds. "*Not yet. Don't kill him—not yet.*"

The transformed Skeleton King cowered on the ground under them, wounded and curled up in the grass.

I walked over to the bow.

There was the red energy—that evil, powerful red energy. It was *in* the bow. That nasty, huge black bow...

It sat in the grass, twice the size of a normal bow, made of glossy, lustrous black wood, with a taught black string that looked like a razor...

My *Chi* felt its red energy coming off in waves...

369

Carefully picking up the powerful magic weapon, I put it into my dimensional pocket, and felt a relief when the *red energy* disappeared.

With my back turned to the group, I suddenly felt a disturbance in my *Chi*.

The Skeleton King exploded into movement, springing to his feet in desperation, and *sprinted* away from us toward the village, gravel spraying from under his bony feet.

"Get him!" WolfBroJake cried, and took a few quick steps, but stopped when I raised a hand.

"*Wait*," I said into their minds. "*Where's he going? Into the village. There's only one way out of there. He won't be able to get over the wall...*"

We followed the fleeing skeleton casually, leaving Xenocide99 behind to guard the exit.

The shrunken Skeleton King ran through the streets, turning down road after road, alley after alley, like a trapped rat, desperate and afraid but with nowhere to go.

The night was coming to an end. The moon was low in the west, and the eastern sky was starting to lighten. If the Skeleton King insisted on running around like a chicken with its head cut off, he wouldn't have long before he'd have to face the daylight...

Eventually, we had the skeleton cornered.

He stood with his back to the northeastern corner of the outer wall, broken arm dangling, eyes alive with fear. The red dots darted around, looking for an escape that didn't exist.

Then he spoke.

"What's going on??" the skeleton cried. "Where am I? Why am I in a village? Why am I hurt? What do you *want* from me??"

"*What are you talking about, Skeleton King?*" I asked into his mind.

The skeleton reached up with thin, bony hands and grasped his skull in surprise.

"What?! Are you in my *head??* What are you doing in my head?!"

371

LuckyMist, WolfBroJake, and I all looked at each other, then back to the Skeleton King.

"*How about you come with us, Skeleton King?*" I asked in his mind.

"Oh man, you *are* talking in my head!!" he exclaimed, clutching his skull even tighter.

"You should come with us," WolfBroJake said. "See the sunshine? You're about to get a whole lot *warmer*, if you know what I mean..."

Reaching out with my *Chi*, I felt the skeleton's mind.

None of the old energy was there. There was no anger. No aggression. Definitely no *red energy*—that was all in the bow, and it was gone now. I could feel this skeleton's mind working hard and working quickly. He was smart, and scared, and confused.

I thought back to when I first saw the Skeleton King; how I felt a strange duality inside his energy:

Something small and strong and intelligent, and something huge and full of spikes and claws and death...

Perhaps the entity of *spikes and claws and death* was gone now, and this creature was the *small and strong and intelligent...*

"*Come with us, skeleton,*" I said, then gestured to the village behind me.

"Okay," he said.

Day 18 – Overworld

Back at the house, the Minecraftians were able to quickly construct a cage for the transformed Skeleton King, by installing iron bars into the corner of the main room.

For a moment, I sensed that the mysterious creature was going to put up a fight, but then, looking around himself at an Enderman ninja and three rough-looking, armored Minecraftians brimming with strength and vitality … he went into the cage willingly.

The Minecraftians were beaming at the thought of returning to their castle, and I couldn't blame them! We had worked hard together to restore the balance of this area, and had suffered a lot trying to defeat the Skeleton King to reclaim their home.

Even though the Minecraftians were probably exhausted, they went to work fixing the broken defensive wall, collecting armor and weapons from the countless bodies of the fallen undead, then they started to break down the 'temporary base' to prepare for the journey home.

For a little while, I sat with the skeleton in the morning.

I would have to return to The End right away to report that my mission was a success and the balance was restored. I'd have to show the evil, magic bow to my master, to determine what he wanted to do with it.

Then, I would probably be released back to my *Seed Stride*, and could help the Minecraftians move back into the castle.

But first, I spoke to the transformed Skeleton King to try and learn more.

"*So who are you?*" I asked into the skeleton's mind.

"I'm Steve," he said. "My name is ... Steve."

Everything he said was shrouded in confusion. His energy, which I felt with my *Chi*, was uncertain all the time!

"*Where do you come from, Steve?*"

"I..." he said, "I was in a castle with an army." Steve shook his head. "No, I was *home*."

"What home? Where is home?"

"Home is to the south ... *no*. Home is ... I ..."

"Why are your eyes red? Was it the bow?"

"My eyes are red?" he asked. He raised a bony hand to his face, then stared at his hand in alarm. Turning it over, watching the bones move as he flexed his fingers, the expression of alarm changed into *horror*. Then he shook his head. "The bow," he said. "The Diabolical Warbow."

"Diabolical Warbow? Is that its name?"

The skeleton nodded.

"Where did it come from? Where did you find the Diabolical Warbow?"

"I've..." he stopped, then thought. "I've *always* had it. At least, I *think* so. No—that couldn't be..."

Eventually, I made my way to the Minecraftians to tell them what I heard from this

Steve, and tell them that I had to warp to The End for a little while. They agreed to wait for me to return before making the journey.

With that, I closed my eyes, mustered my *Chi*, and warped home.

Day 18 – The End

Making my way back to the Temple, I found my master on the roof, and proceeded to tell him the story of the battle, our success, and the strange skeleton and his magical *Diabolical Warbow*.

"*This energy is not of our universe, initiate,*" Master Ee'char said, inspecting the long, smooth lines of the beautiful and wicked black weapon. "*The red energy, as you put it, is the signature of something unnatural and invasive to our worlds, Elias. Something from another universe that is not meant to be here. Wherever you find it, you will find something that will upset the balance…*"

"*Where did it come from, master?*" I asked.

"*I have not felt this before, young one,*" he responded. "*But be careful of this 'Skeleton King' as he is now. If this weapon and its energy was brought here from another universe, and the skeleton is involved still, we must never allow that other universe to connect to ours.*"

"*Why, master?*"

"Their Chi is in direct opposition to the Chi of our worlds. If a portal is created, or if it remains if it already exists, disaster will ensue for our worlds. Disaster for all of us—even here in The End."

"What am I to do now, master?" I asked.

Master Ee'char smiled, his gentle green eyes glowing under the void.

"Initiate Elias," he said, *"I sense that you have finally learned to listen to your Chi. You have learned the Chi Dodge."*

"I believe I have," I said.

"Oh really, initiate?" he responded, laughing in his natural Ender voice. *"You believe you have? Do you know, or do you not know?"*

"My intuition tells me that I know, master," I said.

"Very good, young one. And I sense that you are correct. You are to resume your Seed Stride now. I sense that you would also prefer to go back to Nexus 426, so that you may assist your friends?"

I nodded.

"*Go then, initiate,*" he said. "*But keep the skeleton with you. Take him with you on your Seed Stride, and report to me if you learn anything more about the universe he came from. Be wary of him, Elias. Be wary...*"

"*Yes, master,*" I said, standing.

I bowed, and turned to leave.

"*One more thing, initiate Elias,*" my master said. I turned, and he continued. "*This challenge has been quite sufficient in testing your skills and completing your training in the Chi Dodge. When you return after your Seed Stride, we will make preparations for the trials to test you for the rank of lower ninja.*"

"*Thank you, master,*" I said, then turned away.

Returning to the dragon's island, I watched the great Ender beast flap around in the void while I recharged my *Chi*.

When I was ready, I warped back to the village...

Day 19 – Overworld

By now, I was familiar enough with the village that I could warp directly onto the roof of the Minecraftians' home.

The Overworld was bright, and the glare of the sunlight hurt my eyes after spending time on The End...

I reached up and smoothed my headband.

It occurred to me that I wouldn't be wearing this headband for long. Soon, it would be replaced with another—still the same white novice symbol on the front, but on a *black* band, instead of blue...

Smiling, I meditated for an hour of the Overworld's morning to recharge my *Chi*.

Everything worked out.

The abomination was destroyed. Even though the Skeleton King was not literally *killed*, the red energy that had been warping the skeleton left in his place, the otherworldly *Chi* that had been upsetting the balance of the Overworld … was gone. The *Diabolical Warbow* would now rest in my master's care, back on The End.

Where did it come from? I wondered.

My master had hinted that this skeleton and the bow artifact had come from another universe.

The skeleton *must* have the answer, locked away in his confused and recovering mind…

Below me, I heard the Minecraftians hustling to pack up all of their gear.

Reaching out with my *Chi*, I could sense that they were … *happy*.

All of the conflict and strife they'd gone through over the last several days was *gone*—erased with the defeat of the Skeleton King and the removal of the red energy from Overworld.

And, no doubt, the powers of the beacon made them feel stronger and more vigorous than ever…

An effect I didn't feel anymore, come to think of it.

The immense power that made me feel like a juggernaut and let me cut through the undead army like a whirlwind of death ... was gone.

Turning, I saw that the beacon, the brilliant column of white light, previously piercing the sky from the roof of the village church, wasn't there.

Zip.

On the cobblestone roof of the church, I approached the hole where the beam of light exploded from the attic into the sky before.

Looking down through the opening, I saw that the beacon and the multitude of iron blocks that sat beneath it had been picked up and packed away.

Balder, the master blacksmith, moved around in the dark attic below, cleaning and picking up pieces of debris.

Zip.

I warped down into the empty space.

385

"*Hello, Balder,*" I said into his mind.

The older villager startled at the sound of my teleporting. Tiny purple motes of light lit up the attic interior before fading.

The smith smiled. "*Hello, Enderman,*" he said. "*Welcome back. That was quite a battle you four had!*"

I nodded.

"*We could not have done it without your assistance with the beacon,*" I said in his mind. "*It was the foundation of my plan.*"

He sighed, smiling, and looked at the empty space where the metal pyramid had been.

"*An impressive piece of technology, isn't it?*" Balder asked. "*I've witnessed its power harnessed by the Skeleton King, where it made the skeleton archers move faster than they ever had before. The beacon even brought the Skeleton King himself back from the brink of death! And now, I watched this artifact turn you four into unstoppable killing machines that destroyed an entire army in minutes! Truly impressive...*"

"*Indeed,*" I responded.

"*But we helped each other, ninja,*" the blacksmith went on to say. "*You would have never been able to use the beacon to defeat the Skeleton King if you hadn't rescued me in the first place from the monster's prison! So I thank you, Enderman Elias, for helping me. And helping my apprentice— and this village!*"

Bowing, I said, "*I humbly accept your thanks, blacksmith.*"

I stood quiet for a while, contemplating the last few days since our initial assault on the Skeleton King's army, then I looked down at Balder again.

"*And where is the beacon and its pyramid now?*"

Balder smiled. "*With the Minecraftians, of course! The village has chosen to give it to them. They will be visiting us regularly to trade, after all.*"

"*But all of your iron...?*"

"*A good investment in powerful allies,*" the blacksmith said.

"*I'm sure the Minecraftians will enjoy having the power of the beacon back at their castle...*"

"*Indeed,*" Balder said, then be began fishing through his robes for something. "*You, Elias, on the other hand, were a more difficult puzzle to solve.*"

"*How do you mean?*"

"*As a way to say thank you for defeating the Skeleton King and healing our region, I, and the other villagers, wanted to give you a gift as well.*"

A *gift?* From the villagers?

"*However,*" he said, "*For all of the useful things we could think of to give the Minecraftians, for all of our technology and tools, the puzzle was—what could an Enderman actually appreciate and use?*"

He pulled out a familiar large scroll of paper from his robes.

I paused, and the blacksmith put the large map into my hands.

"*Your...*" I said into his mind. "*Your map?!*"

"*Yes, Ender. My map of the region, filled in with detail of my explorations from these last several years. It's what's known as a 'Level 4 Map', and will accurately depict the land around the village and the castle for a long distance in all directions.*"

"*But Balder,*" I said, "*This is your map. You need it for your mining expeditions—you needed it to escape the Skeleton King's army...*"

"*Yes, I did,*" he responded. "*It's extremely useful. But don't worry, Enderman. I have others. And I can make more. I figured that, even though you are likely to teleport all over when you are on our world, you may want to return here—to our village, to the Minecraftians' castle. So you should have this.*"

I realized that I was trying to gently put the map back into the blacksmith's hands, but when he

389

gave me one last insistent shove, I accepted the gift, and bowed.

"*Thank you, master blacksmith*," I said in his mind. "*I will indeed return here*."

Taking a quick look at the map's detailed and colorful surface, I rolled it back up and placed it into my dimensional pocket.

"*We look forward to seeing you again*," Balder said. "*Now, you should probably meet up with your friends. They have been waiting for you…*"

After catching up with the Minecraftians, who were happy to see me, I found that they had almost entirely broken down the chests, tools, and furniture in their village home. They were saying goodbye to Kumara, who had stopped by, even though they couldn't understand his words in the villager language.

The transformed Skeleton King was also with them, lingering in the back of the group, ready to follow. WolfBroJake had placed one of the dead archers' helmets on his head so that he wouldn't burn in the daylight, and apparently, the Minecraftians had taken to calling him "Skeleton Steve".

"*Skeleton Steve?*" the undead creature asked, thinking for a moment, the red lights in his eyes darting around in thought. "I like it," he said.

Leaving the village, I no longer felt the energy of fear from the villagers. They no longer fled from me.

Following the compass that LuckyMist gave me, the five of us—myself, an Enderman ninja, the three Minecraftians—WolfBroJake, LuckyMist, and Xenocide99, as well as a strange, confused skeleton named *Skeleton Steve*—traveled to the south to reclaim a castle.

From time to time, I pulled out the map that was given to me by Balder, and looked over its beautiful illustrations—the different colors of the grass and the trees, the mountains and snow-capped peaks far in the distance, the strange and interesting blocky structures and layouts of the village just above the center, as well as the castle and the castle grounds and farms to the south. The

Minecraftians looked at it with me. We were all curious, and studied the comparisons between the sketches and the real world around us as we walked.

"Do you think I could have a *bow?*" Skeleton Steve asked. "Just in case ... uh ... I dunno ... we run into trouble??"

Even though the Minecraftians had equipped him with a helmet to protect him against the *daylight*, the skeleton was still unarmed. He never obtained another weapon after I took his *Diabolical Warbow* to The End.

"No way," Xenocide99 said.

"Not a chance," said WolfBroJake. "You might be a wimpy skeleton now, but yesterday you were the Skeleton King!"

"Then *why* am I here?" the strange undead creature asked. "Why didn't you kill me or let me go?"

I had explained to the Minecraftians back in the village that 'Skeleton Steve' had to stay with me on my Seed Stride for the time being, at least until we learned more about him and were sure that he wasn't a threat…

"We're not *monsters*, Skeleton Steve," LuckyMist said.

"*I would like to help you recover your memory, skeleton*," I said into his mind. "*You were clearly corrupted by the artifact weapon. Even though you did terrible things as the Skeleton King, we cannot fault you for just being a vessel for the evil energy of the bow…*"

It was a half-truth.

According to my master, I would have to keep this *Skeleton Steve* close to me. There was no sense in killing him, if he wasn't a threat—especially not if it might be possible to learn more about this dangerous, *red energy* universe if I could help him recover. And I certainly couldn't let him get away if he might pose a further threat to the balance of Overworld, or still held a connection of some kind to a *portal* to the red energy universe…

"Well, gee, thanks," Skeleton Steve said. "How *noble* of you…"

An hour or so after sunset, we finally arrived at the Minecraftians' home. There were a few lost and directionless skeleton archers remaining, but the hardened warriors were able to dispatch them with little effort. Eventually, the Minecraftians were cheering and whooping and making happy sounds as they sprinted around their halls of the huge cobblestone home.

I stood in the courtyard, amidst the sounds of the Minecraftians throwing down chests and emptying their packs inside, and I remembered...

Not far from me was the place where I fell to the Skeleton King. I looked down at the grass. My memory of it was hazy, as I was mortally wounded. At the time, I was trying hard to ignore the army around me and the Skeleton King standing over me. My eyes drifted up to the area of the castle wall, below the battlements and above the balcony roof, where I had teleported to several times—a few times in stealth, and once in desperation while trying to escape death...

LuckyMist suddenly popped into sight, running out onto the balcony from the large bedroom inside.

"Elias!" she exclaimed, waving down at me and smiling. "Come on in!"

Looking down at Skeleton Steve, who stood at my side, I saw the undead creature look back at me impassively. He shrugged.

As long as the transformed Skeleton King was *stuck* with me, I'd have to be more careful about casually teleporting around. Any other day, I would have warped up to the balcony to meet my friend, but if I did that now, I would have to leave this mysterious undead fellow down here in the courtyard.

I walked up to the castle's front doors, and Skeleton Steve followed.

Day 20 – Overworld

The morning sunlight lit up the farm. Rows and rows of wheat had been left to grow wild for the last several days while the Minecraftians were gone. Now, they were golden in the daylight, and waved in the breeze.

I hugged LuckyMist, my long, black arms wrapping around her small form. She hugged me back fiercely, then backed away to stand next to Xenocide99. The warrior put his arm around her.

"Goodbye, Elias," she said. "When will you come back?"

"*Not long,*" I said in their minds. "*I am on my Seed Stride now, and I don't expect to venture far from this region until I return to The End.*"

"When will that be?" WolfBroJake asked.

"*When will I be done with my Seed Stride?*" I asked. "*I don't know. I will know when I am ready, I suppose...*"

"You can always come back whenever you want to, ninja," Xenocide99 said. "In between, or after, or … whatever. You're always welcome here."

The others nodded.

"*Thank you, Minecraftians—my friends*," I said.

After a bit more chatting, I turned to leave with a slight bow.

"Where will you go now?" LuckyMist asked.

"*There is a village on the blacksmith's map, far to the east. I will collect 'seed blocks' on the way there. I am curious to see what another village looks like*…"

After another round of goodbyes, we were off, walking toward the morning sun.

As the skeleton and I walked in silence, I contemplated my lessons from this mission.

The flower.

The ego.

The *Chi Dodge*.

Doing, instead of trying.

"What is that you're writing in?" Skeleton Steve asked me later.

Holding up this book and contemplating the quill held in my slender, black fingers, I said into his mind, "*This is a journal. A diary.*"

"What do you do with it?" he asked, the tiny red dots in his eye cavities pouring over the words I just inked onto the page.

"*Each day, I write about the day's events, and my thoughts. It is the story of my journey. I started writing in this one recently—since just before my first mission. I'm new to the practice.*"

"The story of an Enderman ninja?" Skeleton Steve asked.

I nodded. "*Yes, you could look at it that way. And after the adventure that your 'Skeleton King alter ego' led me on these last several days, I find that I really like it—the writing. I intend to continue.*"

I could see the skeleton's eyes working, staring at the book in my lap. My *Chi* picked up on a torrent of thoughts. Something about my *journal* had seriously piqued his interest...

"That's really cool," Skeleton Steve said. "I think I'd like to try that."

"*It might be a good idea,*" I responded. "*Maybe writing your own journal will help you recover your memory, as well.*"

"The Diary of Skeleton Steve..." the undead creature said, still staring into my book. "The Diary of an Enderman ninja..."

"*I tell you what,*" I said in his mind. "*We'll see if we can find some blank books for you in the library when we reach the next village, okay?*"

His attention snapped back to my face.

"Okay, Enderman," he said.

Extending my *Chi* around me, I felt for the presence of the seeds—the humble beginnings of ender pearls, within the dirt of the Overworld around me.

Stopping, I felt around the ground near a tall pine tree. With my long hands open and receptive, I could detect another seed block...

Somewhere around this tree...

Picking up one dirt block after another, I eventually found the chunk of soil I was looking for.

The dirt block looked like all of the others, but I could *sense* it, like a star in the night sky—the presence of a *new beginning* inside. This pearl seed would grow, in the presence of the dragon, to become a full Ender Pearl, and would one day be joined with an Ender youngling. The *Chi* of the seed beneath the dirt in my hands melded with the *Chi* of my own pearl inside my body, and my pearl felt *warm*...

Smiling, I placed the dirt block into my dimensional pocket.

And we walked on...

Wanna know what happens next??

The story of Elias and Skeleton Steve continues in

"***The Noob Years***" Series!

Check out Episode ONE – It's Free!!

*Love MINECRAFT? **Over 17,000 words of kid-friendly fun!***

This high-quality fan fiction fantasy diary book is for kids, teens, and nerdy grown-ups who love to read epic stories about their favorite game!

The very first diary of Skeleton Steve himself!!

Welcome to a new adventure. Follow along the 'The Noob Years' of Skeleton Steve, Minecraft writer and adventurer, back when he first started his travels on Diamodia! Fresh out of the "Enderman Ninja" series, Skeleton Steve and Elias the Enderman Ninja are traveling east to explore a distant village on the Enderman's map. The village's library is a great place to find an empty journal for Skeleton Steve's first diary, right??

But when the village turns out to be a zombie village, what manner of trouble will the two adventurers run into? And when a mysterious baby zombie offers to give Skeleton Steve the library's last empty book in exchange for finding his missing tome about his "Knight's Code", will Elias and the memory-challenged skeleton be up to the task?

CHECK OUT
SKELETONSTEVE.COM
... to find the NEXT BOOK!

Sign up for my Free Newsletter to get an *email* when the next book comes out!

Go to: www.SkeletonSteve.com/sub

Want More Elias?

1. Please go to where you bought this book and *leave a review!* It just takes a minute and it really helps!

2. Join my free *Skeleton Steve Club* and get an email when the next book comes out!

3. Look for your name under my "*Amazing Readers List*" at the end of the book, where I list my *all-star reviewers*. Heck—maybe I'll even use your name in a story if you want me to! (*Let me know in the review!*)

About the Author - Skeleton Steve

I am *Skeleton Steve*, author of *epic* unofficial Minecraft books. *Thanks for reading this book!*

My stories aren't your typical Minecraft junkfood for the brain. I work hard to design great plots and complex characters to take you for a roller coaster ride in their shoes! Er ... claws. Monster feet, maybe?

All of my stories written by (just) me are designed for all ages—kind of like the Harry Potter series—and they're twisting journeys of epic adventure! For something more light-hearted, check out my "Fan Series" books, which are collaborations between myself and my fans.

Smart kids will love these books! Teenagers and nerdy grown-ups will have a great time relating with the characters and the stories, getting swept up in the struggles of, say, a novice Enderman ninja (Elias), or the young and naïve creeper king

(Cth'ka), and even a chicken who refuses to be a zombie knight's battle steed!

I've been *all over* the Minecraft world of Diamodia (and others). As an adventurer and a writer at heart, I *always* chronicle my journeys, and I ask all of the friends I meet along the way to do the same.

Make sure to keep up with my books whenever I publish something new! If you want to know when new books come out, sign up for my mailing list and the *Skeleton Steve Club*. ***It's free!***

Here's my website:

www.SkeletonSteve.com

You can also 'like' me on **Facebook**:
Facebook.com/SkeletonSteveMinecraft

And 'follow' me on **Twitter**:
Twitter.com/SkeletonSteveCo

And watch me on **Youtube**: (Check my website.)

"Subscribe" to my Mailing List and Get Free Updates!

I *love* bringing my Minecraft stories to readers like you, and I hope to one day put out over 100 stories! If you have a cool idea for a Minecraft story, please send me an email at *Steve@SkeletonSteve.com*, and I might make your idea into a real book. I promise I'll write back. :)

Other Books by Skeleton Steve

The "Noob Mob" Books

Books about individual mobs and their adventures becoming heroes of Diamodia.

SKELETON STEVE

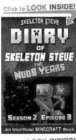

412

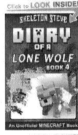
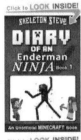

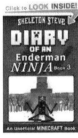

Diary of a Creeper King
Book 1
Book 2
Book 3
Book 4

Skeleton Steve – The Noob Years
Season 1, Episode 1 – ***FREE!!***
Season 1, Episode 2
Season 1, Episode 3
Season 1, Episode 4
Season 1, Episode 5
Season 1, Episode 6
Season 2, Episode 1
Season 2, Episode 2
Season 2, Episode 3
Season 2, Episode 4
Season 2, Episode 5
Season 2, Episode 6
Season 2, Episode 6
Season 3, Episode 1
Season 3, Episode 2
Season 3, Episode 3
Season 3, Episode 4
Season 3, Episode 5
Season 3, Episode 6

Diary of a Teenage Zombie Villager
Book 1 – ***FREE!!***
Book 2
Book 3
Book 4

Diary of a Chicken Battle Steed
Book 1
Book 2
Book 3
Book 4

Diary of a Lone Wolf
Book 1
Book 2
Book 3
Book 4

Diary of an Enderman Ninja
Book 1 – *FREE!!*
Book 2
Book 3

Diary of a Separated Slime – Book 1

Diary of an Iron Golem Guardian – Book 1

The "Skull Kids" Books

A Continuing Diary about the Skull Kids, a group of world-hopping players

Diary of the Skull Kids
Book 1 – *FREE!!*
Book 2
Book 3

The "Fan Series" Books

Continuing Diary Series written by Skeleton Steve *and his fans!* Which one is your favorite?

  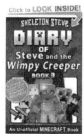

Diary of Steve and the Wimpy Creeper
Book 1
Book 2
Book 3

Diary of Zombie Steve and Wimpy the Wolf
Book 1 *COMING SOON*

The "Tips and Tricks" Books

Handbooks for Serious Minecraft Players, revealing Secrets and Advice

Skeleton Steve's Secret Tricks and Tips

Skeleton Steve's Top 10 List of Rare Tips

Skeleton Steve's Guide to the
First 12 Things I Do in a New Game

Get these books as for FREE!

(**Visit www.SkeletonSteve.com to** *learn more*)

Series Collections and Box Sets

Bundles of Skeleton Steve books from the Minecraft Universe. Entire Series in ONE BOOK.

Great Values! Usually 3-4 Books (sometimes more) for almost the price of one!

Skeleton Steve – The Noob Years – Season 1
Skeleton Steve – The Noob Years – Season 2

Diary of a Creeper King – Box Set 1

Diary of a Lone Wolf – Box Set 1

Diary of an Enderman NINJA – Box Set 1

Diary of the Skull Kids – Box Set 1

Steve and the Wimpy Creeper – Box Set 1

Diary of a Teenage Zombie Villager – Box Set 1

Diary of a Chicken Battle Steed – Box Set 1

Sample Pack Bundles

Bundles of Skeleton Steve books from multiple series! New to Skeleton Steve? Check this out!

Great Values! Usually 3-4 Books (sometimes more) for almost the price of one!

SKELETON STEVE

Skeleton Steve and the Noob Mobs Sampler Bundle
Book 1 Collection
Book 2 Collection
Book 3 Collection
Book 4 Collection

-

Check out the website
www.SkeletonSteve.com
for more!

Enjoy this Excerpt from...

"Diary of Skeleton Steve – The Noob Years" Book 1 (Season 1, Episode 1)

About the book:

Love MINECRAFT? **Over 17,000 words of kid-friendly fun!**

This high-quality fan fiction fantasy diary book is for kids, teens, and nerdy grown-ups who love to read epic stories about their favorite game!

The very first diary of Skeleton Steve himself!!

Welcome to a new adventure. Follow along the 'The Noob Years' of Skeleton Steve, Minecraft writer and adventurer, back when he first started his travels on Diamodia! Fresh out of the "Enderman Ninja" series, Skeleton Steve and Elias the Enderman Ninja are traveling east to explore a distant village on the Enderman's map. The village's library is a great place to find an empty journal for Skeleton Steve's first diary, right??

But when the village turns out to be a zombie village, what manner of trouble will the two adventurers run into? And when a mysterious baby zombie offers to give Skeleton Steve the library's last empty book in exchange for finding his missing tome about his "Knight's Code", will Elias and the memory-challenged skeleton be up to the task?

Love Minecraft adventure??

Read on for an Excerpt for the book!

1 – Beginnings

Where to begin?

Right now I'm sitting on the roof of the watchtower in *Zombietown*, writing in this nice, new journal!

How did I even learn how to write? How do I understand these words? What unknown memories in my undead brain guide my bony fingers to move the quill and ink over these pages?

My name is Skeleton Steve.

Or, at least, that's the name they *gave* me.

I don't know who I am.

I guess a good place to start with would be back when Elias and I were on the road heading to Zombietown. I didn't know it was called 'Zombietown' back then—we gave this place that name later. We just sort of ... started calling it Zombietown. But at the time, it was a Tuesday morning, the square sun was high in the sky, and the forest was bright and beautiful around us.

"So where are we going, again?" I asked.

The tall, black-skinned Enderman walked along beside me, moving in graceful, easy strides. The tails of his blue ninja headband fluttered in the breeze, and the sun glinted on the white symbol over in its center, the symbol of his *ninja order*.

He looked down at me with an unreadable face. His purple eyes glowed.

"*To the east,*" Elias said, his voice inside my head, "*there's a village on the map.*"

It was still very strange to me— communicating with this Enderman via telepathy— speaking inside our heads. The ninja never made a sound otherwise. Never a word, never a *grunt*. The only times he spoke to me was with my *thoughts*, like I was thinking those words myself, in my own voice.

But it *wasn't* my voice. It was his.

"Oh," I responded. "Oh yeah..."

Elias stopped and cocked his head, blocking out the sun for a moment. "*Are you okay? How's your memory?*"

"What a funny question," I replied out loud. The Enderman spoke inside my head, but *I'd* speak out loud. If anyone else was ever watching our conversations, it would look like Elias was staring at me, and I was talking to myself! "*How's your memory?*" I repeated. "If my memory was acting funny, would I have *any* idea?"

We moved on.

"*Valid point, Skeleton Steve,*" he said.

I looked down at my skeletal hands as we walked. Flexed my fingers—watched them open and close.

Who am I? I thought. Who *was* I?

My slender, bony feet crunched through the dirt and grass, and my pack flopped against my hip-bones as I walked. We'd been traveling all morning, following Elias's direction.

Sometimes, the Enderman ninja would stop, and pull his *compass* out of thin air (he called it his *dimensional pocket*), look at the instrument for a moment, glance up at the sun, look up ahead, then, we'd move on...

I realized that this must be very slow for the powerful creature—walking with me like this. I've seen him jump around like magic, *zipping* around using his ... teleportation power. Elias could really cover a lot of ground in a hurry like that!

But ... he wanted to be with me.

To walk with me.

And I appreciated him for it.

Was Elias my friend? I don't know—I didn't even know who I was. Or who I *used* to be. The Enderman claimed that he wanted me to travel with him. He said he wanted to help me get my memories back.

I *guess* he was my friend...

"So what's gonna happen when we find this village?" I asked. "Won't the villagers freak out and not want anything to do with us?"

"*That seems likely,*" Elias replied.

"So ... what's the point??"

"*One reason to go there is to find you a journal, remember?*"

"Well," I said, "wouldn't it make more sense to just go back to the village where you're *already* a hero, and get one there?"

The Enderman looked at me for a moment. I couldn't tell what he was thinking or feeling—not like with the Minecraftians. Those creatures were pretty easy to read. Elias's face however, was just ... *blank*. Black and smooth and blank. With glowing purple eyes that mostly just looked ... gentle and uninterested.

What was going on behind those passive purple eyes? An Enderman *sigh?*

431

"*I have picked up many Ender seeds in the area of the last village already,*" Elias responded. "*It is good to explore, to cover new ground.*"

"Your *Seed Stride?*" I asked. "That's why?"

"*That is one of many reasons, Skeleton King,*" he said. I winced at the name. "*There is also a compelling reason to seek out new villages, and new areas—to become more familiar with this map.*"

The Skeleton King.

Who was the man—the skeleton—that existed *before* the Skeleton King??

My memories from being the monster were almost gone now—just hazy shadows in the back of my mind. At times, when I stayed quiet for too long, I started looking *through* this bright, sunlit world, and caught flashes of an army of skeletal archers; brief glimpses of clashing with this Enderman ninja in mortal battle; quick memories of … *red*…

The Enderman put a slender, black hand on my shoulder.

"*I apologize, Skeleton Steve*," he said. "*I did not mean to use that name...*"

Had I stopped?

Did I stop walking and go into some sort of weird flashback again??

We started moving again.

"It's okay, Elias," I said. "I'm ... sorry too." I shook my skull. "How far do you think the village is?"

"*Well*," the Enderman said, "*From the last time I looked at the map, judging by the time of day, and the plains to the south...*" He pointed to our right and, through the trees, I could see a bright, open area of green grass peppered with yellow and red flowers. "*I surmise that we will be walking for today, and tomorrow, then should reach the unknown village.*"

"Not bad," I said. "You know what?" I looked up at him and smiled.

"*No, I do not*," he responded blankly.

I smirked. Elias was a weird guy. He *definitely* didn't understand that expression. But, how did I??

At every turn, thinking about the mechanics of this … amnesia … seriously boggled my mind. How did I know some things and not others? How did I know how to speak? Or how to use expressions like, *you know what?*

"Err … know what? I kind of *like* this traveling like this," I said.

"That is good, Skeleton Steve," Elias responded. *"This world of Diamodia is immense. It is good to see much of it—to learn much of this place. I have come to understand, from my Seed Stride and my first mission for my order, that there is much self-improvement and growth to be had in journey and adventure…"*

"Journey and adventure, huh?" I asked. "Yeah, I like that."

"Take this creeper for example," Elias said, waving a hand off to our left.

Creeper??

I looked, and didn't see anything. Green. Trees.

And suddenly, a freaking *creeper* stepped out from the woods! Right next to us! Its skin was green like the leaves, and crackly, with four stubby, green legs, and a frowny face with deep, sad eyes like black holes in a dense bush...

"Whoa!" I exclaimed. "Where'd *you* come from?"

"Ssss," the creeper replied. Its voice was dry and scratchy. "I walk through the treesss, ssskeleton!" It approached us and stopped.

"What could you learn from this creature?" Elias went on, in my mind. I had no idea if *only I* heard his mind voice, or if the creeper was hearing it too. *"This creeper may just be another mob, but he has a name, and has been here longer than you have. All of these beings of Diamodia have their own stories—their own lives."*

The creeper stared at us blankly.

"Uh ... *hi there*, creeper!" I said, turning to it. It didn't respond. "What's your name?"

"Cho'thosss," the creeper responded. "Why'sss a *ssskeleton* want to know?"

"Just curious, I guess," I said.

Elias stood by like a silent sentinel, watching our interaction.

This felt weird. What was the Enderman trying to do? Make me have a conversation with the creeper?

The creeper suddenly looked up at Elias, and watched his face for a while.

"Yesss, Ender," the creeper said. "There'sss a cassstle to the wessst. What'sss with hisss eyesss? They glow *red!*" It glanced at me with its sad, deep eyes, then turned back to Elias.

They looked at each other's faces for a while longer. Elias must have been talking to the creeper with his *mind voice*, and I wasn't a part of the conversation...

"Not that I know of," Cho'thos responded, its voice like leaves and gravel. "I have not gone much farther eassst..."

436

The Enderman ninja gave the creeper a small nod.

"Good travelsss," the creeper said to both of us, then walked around us, continuing to the south.

"Uh … nice to *meet* you, Cho'thos!" I said after him. I looked at Elias. "What was *that* about? Asking him about the village?"

"*Yes*," my companion replied. "*He's familiar with this area, and the Minecraftians' castle, but hasn't been much further east than we are now.*"

"Yeah, I got some of that," I said, and we walked on for a while.

When the sun went down and the world became dark, Elias insisted that we stop for the night. Neither of us needed to sleep, but the Enderman preferred to stop at night to meditate and recharge his *Chi*—whatever *that* was.

We both sat in a small clearing between tall oak trees, and I watched the Enderman as he sat straight, crossed his legs, and put a slender hand on each knee. Appearing very serene, Elias closed his eyes, and stayed like that for the rest of the night. Only the blue tails of his ninja headband moved, drifting up and down in the night breeze.

I sat in the dark, watching and listening to the strange world around me, wondering if those zombies and spiders I heard and saw in the distance ever had a taste for *bones*...

2 – On the Road

When the square moon set, and the sun brightened the day again, we continued our journey.

Elias stopped every once and a while to do his weird Enderman stuff.

His *Seed Stride*.

Sometimes, gliding along like the long and limber creature from another world he was, Elias would stop, close his eyes, then head off of our path a bit, holding his hands out in front of him. With those powerful and lean arms, he'd dig his fingers into the dirt, and pull up a block or two. Occasionally, he'd have to dig and set aside *block after block* until he found the dirt block he was looking for...

They all looked the same to me.

But Elias sure acted *funny* about those blocks, treating *some* of them like they were nothing interesting at all (*they weren't interesting*

439

of course—*just dirt*), and others like they were full of *diamonds* or something! His eyes would flare, and he'd look over those 'special' dirt blocks like they were the coolest things he'd ever seen. And then, he'd slip them away into nothing—into his *dimensional pocket*.

"What do you see in those?" I asked, eventually.

The Enderman was regarding one of those 'special' blocks. He held it up for me to see, treating it with gentle care.

"*Behold*," Elias said. "*What do you see?*"

Dirt.

It was a block of dirt.

"Just looks like dirt," I said.

"*Inside this dirt*," he replied, "*is an 'Ender Seed'—something sacred to my people.*"

"Like, some kind of ... *egg?*" I asked.

"*Not exactly*," Elias said. "*Each of us Ender has an Ender Pearl inside, which is an amplifier for our Chi, and allows us to channel much of our power into the techniques you have seen me use—my ability to warp, my mind voice, and other, more subtle things."*

"And they come from *dirt?*"

"This world, Diamodia, has three connected planes. Do you know of them?"

"What are *planes?*"

"The End, which is my home, the Nether, and this world—the Overworld. All are planes, like worlds within a world."

"What's that have to do with the dirt??"

"All planes are connected, and are vital to each other. We Ender, who live in The End, rely on the Overworld to produce the Ender Seeds, which grow naturally in the soil of the world. When my people go on our Seed Strides, we collect the seeds to bring back to the dragon's island, where they will grow into new pearls for Ender younglings."

Dragon??

"Um … dragon island? Is there a dragon??"

"*The Ender Dragon*," Elias replied. "*The ancient beast bound to my people's civilization that grows the pearls*."

"Can I *see* the dragon?" I asked.

"*Perhaps, one day, I will lead you to The End. But, for an Overworld-dweller like yourself, that would be a very involved adventure. You cannot reach The End as easily as I can*."

"Can't you just *teleport* us there?"

Elias seemed to smile. "*I can return there at will*," he said. "*But I cannot take you with me*."

As we walked, I listened to spiders hissing and climbing around in the trees around us. Looking up, I watched their multiple, glowing red eyes regard us from the shadows.

"Um … Elias?" I asked.

"*I sense that you are distressed about the mobs around us*," he said in my mind. "*You do not need to fear*."

"Do you think I could at least ... have a weapon?? A bow or something? I mean—I know the Minecraftians didn't want me to have one, but they're long behind us now, you know?"

The memory echoed in my head:

"Do you think I could have a bow?" I asked. "Just in case ... uh ... I dunno ... we run into trouble??"

"No way," Xenocide99 said.

"Not a chance," said WolfBroJake. "You might be a wimpy skeleton now, but yesterday you were the Skeleton King!"

My first memories of transforming into a normal skeleton after being ... that *monster* ... were kind of hazy, but I could still remember the Minecraftians and Elias standing around me, as I waited in my cage for them to decide on my fate...

I was truly grateful that this Enderman spoke up and didn't allow the Minecraftians to *execute* me. They sure had every right to...

"*Why do you feel the need to have a weapon?*" Elias asked.

"What if those spiders attack?"

Elias shook his head, and looked up into the trees. He stared at the individual arachnids handing out in the upper branches as we walked on. After a while, he looked down at me again, then pointed at one of them. The spider's glowing red eyes glared down at me.

"*That spider's name is Sidney. He's up there because he likes to spend the day in the sunshine at the top of the trees. He feels happy and warm.*" Elias pointed to another. "*That one's name is Sophia. Sidney's her best friend, so she hangs out with him a lot, and is hoping they're going to go explore a certain cave nearby after lunch.*"

"Okay … what about that one?" I asked, pointing at a third.

"What *about* me?!" the spider called down from above with a hissing voice.

"*That's Seth,*" Elias said. "*He just wanted to see what the other two were doing up there.*"

I felt a bit silly.

"Oh, *nothing* … Seth. Have a nice day!"

"You too, bones!" Seth replied.

"Hey, you guys!" the spider named Sophia cried out in a spidery voice. "Watch out for the Minecraftians! There are a *bunch* of them living nearby!"

She must have meant the Minecraftians in the castle *behind* us.

"Thanks!" I said, and we walked on.

"You don't have much to fear from other mobs here, Skeleton Steve," Elias said. *"Don't forget—you are one of them, yourself!"*

"Still," I said. "I'd like to have a weapon. If something bad happens, what am I gonna do? You have your awesome ninja skills, but I'm just … I'm just a bunch of bones."

"Soon," the Enderman replied. *"Be patient, Skeleton Steve. You are still recovering from being*

... the other. We must make sure that ... your state of mind is safe."

We walked in silence for a while.

"What was I, Elias?" I asked. "What was the Skeleton King? Who am I now? Was I *always* the Skeleton King before?"

Elias shook his head. *"I do not believe you were always the Skeleton King, Skeleton Steve,"* he said. *"From what I could tell, you were ... distorted ... by a magical artifact—an evil magical item that is no longer on this plane. I feel rather certain that you were something else, or someone else, before the artifact made you into the Skeleton King."*

"Can you show me?" I asked.

"Show you what?"

"With your *mind power*. Can you make me see myself, as the Skeleton King, from your own memories, maybe?"

"That is an odd request, Skeleton Steve," Elias responded. *"Why would you want to*

446

remember being the Skeleton King? That's not who you are now..."

"Maybe it'll help me remember who I was—you know—before!"

"*Are you sure?*" the Enderman said. "*I could send you ... images, short memories, I suppose. But will it really help you? It will likely cause you pain.*"

"Please," I said. "I *want* to see."

Elias stopped, and we stood in tall grass.

The monster stood in the room directing his skeleton minions as they carried more of the heavy metal blocks over from a corner of the room. In the shadows, spared from the red light, I caught a glint of steel.

Were the blocks made of solid iron?

My eyes darted back to the Skeleton King.

The abomination stood twice as tall as the skeletons around him—taller than me. And he was thick and wide, with heavy ribs and dense limbs. The Skeleton King's bones were overall more massive than normal skeleton bones, and he had a broad lower jaw that made him appear even more menacing. As I expected, his eyes held the same fierce, red pinpricks of glowing light as the other skeletons. The monster's shoulders were armored, and he held a huge, black bow in one chunky bone hand.

No ... not in his hand. On his hand!

The Skeleton King was armed with a great, black bow that was bolted sideways onto a bracer of some kind that was attached to his right arm.

"Move it!" he yelled, his voice like thunder. "Get those blocks in there!"

The skeletal minions struggled with the heavy blocks to finish their work on the pyramid.

I shook my head.

That was weird. I was suddenly aware of the tall grass around me again. Elias stood before me, regarding me with a passive, smooth face and glowing purple eyes. I looked up at the blue sky above me and felt the sunshine on my face.

"*Are you alright?*" Elias asked. "*Did you see?*"

"I..." Pausing, I tried to collect my thoughts. "*That* was weird. I was suddenly ... in a castle? The Minecraftians' castle??"

"*Did that ... stir any memories?*" Elias asked. "*Did the monster feel like you?*"

Nothing.

"No, not really. I was just seeing the Skeleton King from *your eyes*. It didn't *feel* like me. Can you do it again, maybe a ... *stronger* memory??"

Elias pressed his hands together. He seemed resistant to the idea, although I couldn't read his strange, Enderman face for the life of me...

"*Very well,*" he said, and my mind was swooped away into a ... flying kick!

Flying through the air, I visualized my kick hitting the Skeleton King in the center of his chest. Then, just as my foot was about to connect, I was shocked when the Skeleton King's massive ribcage

449

split apart up the center and opened up like a sideways chest—like a great clam-shell trap—and my body crumpled inside of it!

The ribcage trap slammed shut on me, crushing me inside the abomination's body.

Pain...

I cried out, and roared in agony!

The Skeleton King's chest was large enough that such an attack would have totally swallowed up a Minecraftian. But I, as an Enderman, was too big to be completely enclosed, so I was tangled up in a deathtrap of bones, crushed, stuck...

Then, the ribcage opened up and spat me back out onto the ground.

I landed in the dirt, feeling broken.

Trying to get to my feet, I barely noticed the Skeleton King raise his bow to me again.

Zip.

I teleported just a few feet away as he fired, the black arrow hitting the ground where I was.

When I appeared, I collapsed onto the ground again.

Clunk clunk clunk clunk clunk clunk clunk. The skeleton army around us beat their bones in a constant rhythm song of hand-to-hand combat...

I was exhausted and broken.

The Skeleton King turned, and raised his bow again.

Fired.

The black arrow pierced my chest and almost pinned me to the ground! The pain was unbelievable...

"Give me the beacon!" the Skeleton King roared.

I could barely see.

Clunk clunk clunk clunk clunk clunk clunk.

Looking up at him, I tried to get to my feet, then fell again.

"Give me the beacon or DIE!!" the *abomination bellowed.*

I heard the voice repeating in my head...

Die...

Die...

Die...

When I came to, Elias was trying to help me stand from the ground. I was sprawled out in the grass, holding my chest. The huge, black arrow that pinned me to the ground was...

Wait.

There *was* no black arrow...

That was from a memory that wasn't mine.

And that's all it was.

The Skeleton King was a terrible monster, but he wasn't me at all!

Seeing the abomination wiping the floor with Elias, from the ninja's point of view, was *horrifying*, but it didn't remind me of anything.

452

Seeing that massive, menacing creature was no different than ... if he was standing in front of me as ... something else...

It was all very confusing, but it didn't help at all.

"Oh ... that's ... oh my—" I stammered as the Enderman helped me to my feet.

"*Are you okay, Skeleton Steve?*" he asked, his *mind voice* serious and concerned.

"Elias ... I'm ... *are you??* That was terrible! How did you ... I'm *so sorry!*"

"*I am okay now,*" Elias replied. "*I will always have the scars from my battles with your other form, but the Skeleton King was also a great mentor to me, in its way, and helped me grow as a ninja.*"

"I'm sorry, Elias," I said. "The ... weapons ... never mind. I'm sure I'll be fine. I've got *you*, after all. Just ... whenever you think I'm ready? A bow or something?"

Not much later, just as the sun was setting in the western sky behind us, we saw the distant lights of torches across a darkening plateau.

The village…

"*Skeleton Steve,*" Elias said. "*We will rest here, and approach in the morning, after I have recharged my Chi…*"

"Okay, Elias," I said, my thoughts still on the terrible memories from the Enderman's mind.

So, my memories of being the Skeleton King probably won't help me. I had to remember who I was *before* I became the monster! But, since the moment I became a normal skeleton again, I couldn't remember *anything* from before!

Who was I before?? Just a random skeleton?

Hopefully starting a journal would help me to remember…

3 – Zombietown

We approached the village in the morning with caution.

After all, the villagers wouldn't know us from any other random skeletons and Endermen out there. They wouldn't know that Elias was a *hero*, an ally to Balder's village—Balder was the blacksmith who gave the ninja his map. They wouldn't realize that he was a friend of the Minecraftians—the *hero Enderman ninja* who saved the village from … well … from *me*…

Elias figured that we should scout out the village real quiet-like. There was also the possibility that some *other* Minecraftians lived here, and they probably wouldn't be friendly.

"*I'm not sensing any villager energy,*" the Enderman said in my mind. "*Nothing Minecraftian, either.*"

"So what's out there? What's going on?" I asked.

"Let's find out," my companion replied.

The closer we came to the village, the stranger it seemed. Even though it *looked* like a normal village, there was something … *off* about it.

There were no crops. The farming fields were empty—rows of bare dirt with troughs full of water in between.

And there were no villagers.

No bustling, energetic, always-moving-around villager creatures. No constant opening and closing of doors.

Instead, the people we saw standing in the streets … were zombies!

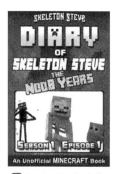

CHECK OUT
SKELETONSTEVE.COM
... to CONTINUE READING!

Currently FREE!!

Enjoy this Excerpt from...
"Diary of a **Lone Wolf**" Book 1

About the book:

Dakota was a young wolf, happy with his life in a wolf pack in the taiga forest where he was born.

Almost fully-grown, Dakota was fast and loved to run. He had friends, loved his mother, respected his alpha, and had a crush on a young female pack-mate.

But his life was about to change forever when his pack was attacked by *the Glitch*, a mysterious and invincible horde of mobs that appeared and started killing everything in their path!

Now, he was a **lone wolf**. With the help of Skeleton Steve, would he ever belong to another pack again? Would they escape *the Glitch* and warn the rest of Diamodia?

Love Minecraft adventure??

Read on for an Excerpt for the book!

Day 1

So how does a *wolf* tell a story? What should I say, Skeleton Steve?

Oh? Where should I start?

Okay.

So, I guess, my name is *Dakota*. I'm a wolf.

Heh ... I already said that. I guess, technically, I'm a *dog* now. No? Doesn't matter?

Skeleton Steve is telling me that I'm a wolf. *Steve* calls me a dog. But I don't understand much about what *Steve* says.

Is this confusing? I'm sorry. Where was I?

Just from ... okay, right before.

Well, I guess I can start by telling you about my old pack. My family.

Just a few days before the attack, it was a day like any other.

I woke up in the forest and leapt to my feet! It was a *beautiful* morning. The forest was in shadows of the rising sun, a cool breeze was crisp on my face, and I could smell the woods come alive! Approaching a tall pine tree, I scratched my shoulders on its bark.

All of my pack was waking up around me.

What a great life!

I ran down to the creek, and drank some water. Splashed my face into it. *Cold!* And shook my fur, sending drops of cold mountain water all over before bounding back up the hill.

I guess it's a good time to introduce *the pack*.

My eyes went first to the alpha and his mate. Logan and Moon. Logan was a huge wolf, and he was really nice. He and Moon didn't talk with us very much, but he was a good leader. Logan mostly kept to himself, quiet and strong, and he led us through the mountains day by day whenever we moved.

Right now, we'd spent the last several days hanging out *here*. There were fields full of sheep nearby, and with this nice, flat area, a mountain creek down the hill a bit, and plenty of shade, it was a good clearing to stay in for a while. I was sure we'd move on soon. We always did.

My belly rumbled. We didn't eat yesterday. Today, I knew the alpha would probably send Archie and me to scout out another herd of sheep for the pack to hunt. I was so *fast*, one of the fastest wolves in the pack, and Archie was pretty fast too, so Logan usually sent us out to find the food.

I loved my job! It was great, roaming around with my best bud, running as fast as we could, exploring the mountains all around the clearing where the pack lived. It was only last year when I was finally old enough to be given a job to do. I loved being able to help my family so well.

Taking a big breath of fresh air, I looked around at the rest of the pack waking up and frolicking in the brisk morning.

Over at the edge of the forest were Colin and Arnou. They were the *warriors*, really. We all help each other, and we all have shared tasks given to us by the alpha, but the big and muscular brothers, Colin and Arnou, were really great at fighting, and they were always the first to defend the pack against any mobs that attacked us—the first aside from *Logan the alpha*, that is.

There was my mother, Minsi, one of the older female wolves. I loved my mother. She sat on her own this morning, watching the birds and chewing on a bone.

Running and playing together was the mated pair, Boris and Leloo. Leloo helped raise the cubs (all of the females did, really), and Boris, along with his brother Rolf, were very good at hunting and taking down our prey. The two hunter brothers were very skilled at circling a herd of sheep or other food, and making the animals run whichever way they wanted.

Sitting in the shadow of a couple of pine trees were Maya, and her daughter, Lupe.

Lupe was my age.

She was a beautiful wolf. And smart too. And funny.

I dunno. For some reason, I had a really hard time *talking* to her. Archie joked with me a lot that I should make her my mate, but whenever I walked up to her, whenever I tried to talk to her, my tongue became stupid, I forgot was I wanted to say, and I just embarrassed myself whenever I tried.

It was terrible! Yes, I guess, I really, really liked her. It should have been easy!

Easy just like with Logan and Moon. Logan has been alpha since before I was born, but my mother told me that before he was alpha, when he was younger, he just walked up to Moon one day and *decided* that they were going to be mates.

I don't really understand how that works. Maybe one day I will.

"Hey, dude!" said Archie, running up to see me.

"Oh, hey! Good morning!" I said, sitting in the dirt.

Archie was a year older than me, and my best friend. When we were growing up, we always did everything together. And now that we were practically adult wolves (almost), we worked together whenever Logan gave us an assignment.

"You ready?" he said, wagging his tail.

"Ready for what?" I asked.

"Going to look for a herd, of course!" he replied.

"Well, yeah, but Logan hasn't told us to yet."

"I bet he will," Archie said.

Not an hour went by before the massive alpha called on us.

"Dakota! Archie!" he said, his deep voice clear above the rest of the pack, chatting in the morning. We ran up and sat before him.

"Yes, sir?" we said.

"You two explore down in the valley today, see if you can find another herd for us to hunt."

"Right away," I said. Archie acknowledged as well, and we departed our pack's temporary home, flying down the hill as quickly as our speedy wolf feet would take us. With the wind in my face, I dodged around trees, leapt over holes, exploded through the underbrush, and felt great!

When we emerged from the huge, pine forest, I felt the sun warm up my face, and I closed my eyes, lifting my snout up into the sky. Archie popped out of the woods next to me.

"Look at that," Archie said. "Have you ever seen anything so beautiful?"

The sunshine on our faces was very pleasant, and looking down, I could see a huge grassy field, full of red and yellow flowers. Little bunnies hopped around here and there, and in the distance was a group of sheep—mostly white, one grey, one black.

Beautiful. I thought of *Lupe*.

"Awesome," I said. "And hey—there's the sheep over there!"

We returned to the pack and led everyone through the forest back to the colorful and sunny meadow we found.

Soon, we were all working together to keep the sheep in a huddle while Logan, Boris, and Rolf, darted into the group of prey and eventually took them all down. After Logan and Moon had their fill, the rest of us were free to eat what we wanted.

I chomped down on the raw mutton and filled my belly. The sun was high, a gentle breeze blew through the meadow, and I felt warm and happy. Archie ate next to me, and I watched Lupe from afar, dreaming of a day when I would be brave enough to *decide* she was my mate.

Life was good.

Day 2

Today Archie and I went for a swim.

It wasn't necessary to go looking for more food yet, according to the alpha, so we were instructed to stay together, for the most part.

As a pack, we didn't eat every day. But sometimes, I got lucky and found a piece of rotten zombie flesh on the ground after the undead mobs burned up in the morning. Today wasn't one of those days, but it happened *sometimes*.

Anyway, it was fortunate that the mountain creek was just down the hill. Archie and I were able to run down and swim, while the rest of the pack sat around digesting all of the mutton we ate yesterday.

A section of the creek was nice and deep, so my friend and I splashed around and competed to see who could dog-paddle the longest. Archie won most of those times, but I know that I'm *faster* than him on the ground, ha ha.

There was a bit of a commotion around lunchtime when my mother happened upon a skeleton archer that was hiding in the shadows under a large pine tree. She gasped and back-pedaled as the undead creature raised his bow and started firing arrows into our midst.

Arnou was nearby, and responded immediately, with Colin close behind.

As the warrior wolves worked together to flank the skeleton, the mob did get *one* decent shot off, and Colin yelped as an arrow sank into his side. But the two strong wolves lashed out quickly, and were able to latch onto the skeleton's arms and legs, taking him down in no time. Only bones remained.

Colin and Arnou each took a bone, and went back to their business of lounging with the pack.

"Are you okay?" I said to my mother.

"Yes, thank you, Dakota," she said. "I'm glad you were out of the way."

"Oh come on, mom," I said. "I could have taken him."

"I know you could have, sweetie," she replied, and licked my face.

I don't know why the skeleton attacked. Sometimes the mobs attacked us. Sometimes not. Sometimes we (especially Colin and Arnou) attacked *them*. We did *love* zombie meat and skeleton bones, but I've never felt the urge to outright *attack* one of the undead to get it. I knew that if we were patient, we would always find more sheep and get plenty to eat.

Later that day, Archie caught me staring at Lupe, and decided to give me a hard time.

"You should go and *talk* to her, man!" he said, nudging me with his snout in her direction. Lupe noticed the movement, and looked over at us. I saw her beautiful, dark eyes for an instant, and then I turned away.

"Cut it out, man! Jeez!" I shoved him back with my body. "You made her look!"

"So what?" he said. "What's wrong with looking?" He laughed. "Maybe she *should* look. Then something will finally *happen*!"

I stole a glance back to her from the corner of my eye. She had looked away, and was laying in the grass again, looking at the clouds as they rolled by. Usually she hung out around her mother, Leloo, but she was by herself for the moment.

Could I? Did I dare?

"Look, dude," Archie said. "She's by herself. *Go for it!*"

I gulped, and looked back at my friend. I looked around at all of the other pack members. They weren't paying any attention. Just going about their own things.

Padding silently through the grass, I approached. Quiet. Well, not *too* quiet. Didn't want to look like I was sneaking up on her! I just didn't want to look *loud*. Okay, I needed to be a *little* louder.

Snap. Crunch. I made some random noises on the ground as I approached.

Jeez, I thought. *I'm being a total weirdo! What am I doing?*

Lupe turned her head to my approach, and when I saw her face, my heart fluttered.

"Hi, Dakota!" she said.

She was happy. Good. I wanted to see her happy. Make her happy. Umm … if she *wanted* to be happy. Then I'd help her be happy. *What?*

"Oh … hi," I said. Gulped.

She watched. Smiled. Waited patiently. What would I say? I couldn't really think of anything.

"How's it going?" she asked.

"Good. *Great!*" I said. "*Really* great!"

"That's cool," she replied.

I looked back, and saw Archie watching. He nudged at me with his nose from far away. *Go on*, he said without words.

"Uh," I said, "How are you?"

Lupe smiled and looked back at the clouds.

"Oh, I'm fine, thanks." Her tail gave a little wag.

"So, uh," I said, trying to think of something to talk about. "Did you get plenty of mutton yesterday? Lots to eat? I hope you ate a lot! *I mean*—not that it looks like you eat a lot, or too much. I mean—you're not *fat* or anything; I didn't think you look fat—"

Her face contorted in confusion.

Holy heck! What was I doing?

"Um … I'm sorry! I'm not calling you fat I just … uh …"

Lupe laughed a nervous laugh.

"Ah … yeah," she said. "I got plenty to eat. Thanks to *you*."

"Um … me, and *Archie*. We found the sheep."

"Yeah, she said. "I know." She smiled, then watched the clouds.

476

"Yeah," I responded. I watched her, trying to think of something to say that wasn't completely *boneheaded*. After a few moments, she noticed me *staring*, and looked back at me. I looked up to the sky.

Her tail gave a small wag.

"Okay, well," I said, "I guess I'll go see how Archie is doing."

"Oh, really?" she asked. "Well, okay, I guess..."

"Okay," I said. "Well, bye."

"Bye," she said, gave me a smile, then looked back to the clouds she was watching.

I walked back to my friend feeling like an idiot, being careful not to walk like a weirdo.

Later that night, I laid in the grass, watching the stars. As the square moon moved across the sky, I looked at a thousand little pinpricks of light, shining and twinkling far, far away, drifting through space.

Most of the pack was already asleep. I could see Lupe sleeping next to her mom. Archie was sleeping near me, and the rest of the pack kept close together—my mother, the warriors and hunters, Leloo. The alphas slept away from us, a little ways up the hill.

The night was quiet, aside from the occasional zombie moan far in the distance, or the hissing of spiders climbing the trees. I was a little hungry, but tried to ignore my belly.

The stars all looked down at me from the vast, black sky, watching over all of us. So pretty.

Day 3

The morning started like all others.

We woke up and the pack was abuzz with hunger. It would be another scouting day for Archie and me. I ran down to the creek to splash cold water on my face, and found a piece of zombie flesh.

Even though I was hungry, I decided not to eat it. I took the delicious piece of meat in my mouth, careful not to sink my teeth into its sweet and smelly goodness, and brought it to my mom.

"Aw, *thanks*, honey!" she said. "Do you want to split it with me?"

"No, that's okay, mom. You have it," I said.

"But you're probably going to go looking for a herd with Archie today, right? You should take some and have the energy."

"That's alright, mom. I'll eat later."

"Okay, but I'll hang onto half of it in case you change your mind, okay?" She started to eat the zombie meat.

As we expected, Logan called on Archie and I to go out and find another herd of sheep. We happily complied, and ran through the forest for the better part of an hour, seeking out prey for the pack.

It was a warm day, and the breeze in my face felt great! My feet were fast, and the forest smelled good, and I ran like the wind. After a while, I caught the scent of mutton, and led Archie to a small herd of sheep wandering around in dense trees.

"There's our meal ticket!" Archie said. "Let's go back!"

"Let's *do it!*" I said, and we laughed as we sprinted through the woods back to the pack.

After dodging through the trees, leaping over boulders, and running silently through the straights like grey ghosts, we approached the forest clearing where the pack was living.

But something was *wrong*.

As we came down the hill, past enough trees to see the clearing, I smelled a weird smell. Something different that I hadn't smelled before. Something *alien*. And as we approached closer, I heard the sounds of battle!

Zombies moaned and growled. Skeletons clattered. Bows twanged, and arrows whistled through the air. I heard growls and scratches, thumps and crashes. Yelps and cries and raw wolf snarls!

"What the—?" Archie cried, as we ran down to the clearing.

Our pack was *fighting for their lives* against a group of zombies and skeletons!

I couldn't count how many of the undead were down there—the scene was confusing. For some reason, the battle was taking place in *broad daylight*, and the mobs weren't burning up in the sun!

In the chaos before us, I had a very hard time making out who was alive and who was already dead. The alpha was obviously still alive, running to and fro between the undead, striking with power and mainly pulling the attackers off of the other wolves. Moon, I think, was doing the same. Several wolves lay dead. My stomach suddenly turned cold...

CHECK OUT
SKELETONSTEVE.COM
... to CONTINUE READING!

The Amazing Reader List

Thank you SO MUCH to these Readers and Reviewers! Your help in leaving reviews and spreading the word about my books is SO appreciated!

Awesome Reviewers:

MantisFang887 EpicDrago887

ScorpCraft SnailMMS WolfDFang

LegoWarrior70

Liam Burroughs

Ryan / Sean Gallagher

Habblie

Nirupam Bhagawati

Ethan MJC

Jacky6410 and Oscar

MasterMaker / Kale Aker

Cole

Kelly Nguyen

Ellesea & Ogmoe

K Mc / AlfieMcM

JenaLuv & Boogie

Han-Seon Choi

Danielle M

Oomab

So Cal Family

Daniel Geary Roberts

Jjtaup

Addidks / Creeperking987

D Guz / UltimateSword5

TJ

Xavier Edwards

DrTNT04

UltimateSword5

Mavslam

Ian / CKPA / BlazePlayz

Dana Hartley

Shaojing Li

Mitchell Adam Keith

Emmanuel Bellon

Melissa and Jacob Cross

Wyatt D and daughter

Jung Joo Lee

Dwduck and daughter

Yonael Yonas, the Creeper Tamer (Jesse)

Sarah Levy / shadowslayer1818

Pan

Phillip Wang / Jonathan55123

Ddudeboss

Hartley

Mitchell Adam Keith

L Stoltzman and sons

D4imond minc4rt

Bookworm_29

Tracie / Johnathan

Jeremyee49

Endra07 / Samuel Clemens

And, of course ... Herobrine

(More are added all the time! Since this is a print version of this book, check the eBook version of the latest books—or the website—to see if your name is in there!)

Made in the USA
Middletown, DE
09 May 2020

94211144R00293